THE COUNTRY DECORATOR

COUNTRY LIVING
MAGAZINE

THE COUNTRY DECORATOR

MIRANDA INNES

HESTER PAGE   GEORGINA RHODES

EBURY PRESS
LONDON

This book is dedicated to all those whose energy and imagination formed the raw material and whose efforts make the world a more attractive place.

First published in 1994

1 3 5 7 9 10 8 6 4 2

First published in the United Kingdom in 1994 by Ebury Press,

Random House, 20 Vauxhall Bridge Road, London SW1V 2SA

Random House Australia (Pty) Limited, 20 Alfred Street, Milsons Point,

Sydney, New South Wales 2061, Australia

Random House New Zealand Limited, 18 Poland Road, Glenfield,

Auckland 10, New Zealand

Random House South Africa (Pty) Limited, PO Box 337, Bergvlei, South Africa

Random House UK Limited Reg. No. 954009

A CIP catalogue record for this book is available from the British Library

ISBN: 0 09 178349 6

Designer: GEORGINA RHODES
Editor: JOANNA BRADSHAW
Locations and Picture Editor: HESTER PAGE
Picture Research: CLAIRE WORTHINGTON

Typeset by Richard Proctor, London

Printed and bound in Italy by New Interlitho S.p.a, Milan

CONTENTS

FOREWORD

Editing a magazine that is chiefly concerned with house decoration and design is simultaneously a joy and a nightmare. Being given licence to look further than just through the windows of a beautiful Georgian rectory or thatched cottage is extremely satisfying to someone of an inquisitive (some might say just plain nosey) nature like myself. But then when such stunning photographs of these beautiful homes appear on the pages of Country Living, I feel a severe sense of inadequacy.

That is how this book was born. Readers would covet these effects too, and would write to ask how that particular paint finish was done, or how that floor was painted, or why that living room looked casually chic when theirs looked plain dowdy? It was obvious that all the information had to be put into one volume.

So here, at last, is the definitive manual on creating exciting but comfortable surroundings. The team who have put the book together could not be better qualified: Hester Page, Country Living's innovative houses editor has that rare "eye" for design so much envied by the rest of us. With Miranda Innes' brilliant text and Georgina Rhodes' intelligent art direction they have together created a practical guide to decorating your home in the country style. You will not, I am pleased to say, find pages of over-swagged curtains, and gilt furniture, but you *will* find comfortable and easy-to-live in rooms for families who live real lives with children, dogs and cats. This is a book that is not only beautiful to look at, but also a classic of the future: the essential manual on Country Decorating.

Francine Lawrence
Editor, *Country Living* Magazine

INTRODUCTION

*F*ortunately, Country Decorating is not just about the country. It is an unspecific term which springs to life as an alternative to urban decor. Somehow the city conjures up the briefly fashionable, the designer commodity, speedy obsolescence and an embarrassing stigma attached to anything that is moments beyond its sell-by date.

By contrast, the most beloved country essentials are those pieces of furniture or objects that have been in the family for generations, or look as if they have. In the country, anything brand-new evokes a blush; state-of-the-art is a phrase spoken *sotto voce* if at all; and the comforting and enduring appeal of the natural is what informs the general atmosphere.

A natural style may be derided by fashion victims, but it never fails to look good. Simple fabrics like ticking, calico and muslin have a casual, effortless style; while plain, solid pine furniture with a peasant past, unadorned but for a wash of translucent colour, will always radiate serene adaptability. Country decorating relies on an absence of pretension, a dearth of fussy wallpaper, a complete lack of festoon, Austrian, or balloon blinds and a studied exclusion of marquetry, parquetry, or veneer on spindly legs.

If actual period authenticity is a little difficult to achieve, then authenticity of mood and spirit is easier and less costly. For example, you may aspire to ancient worn flagstones, but seagrass is more manageable and has a kindly affinity for bucolic life. In your heart of hearts, you may hanker for brocade, but coarse Indian crewel embroidery, while not indigenous, has a rustic soul.

The point is to enjoy a relaxed and pleasurable life surrounded by things you like. People, animals and occasions come first, while objects – even your great-grandmother's pieced quilt – should come some way down the list in importance. Objects are there to be used and to give pleasure: life is too short to spend it hoarding and worrying. If you happen to own Horatio Nelson's trouser press and it is an object of supreme ugliness, do yourself a favour and pass it on to some real enthusiast via one of the auction houses – ditto the gloomy Wedgwood bequeathed by your aunt and anything else you keep because you think you ought to.

But a country look need not be spartan – bare boards and white walls are one approach, and a calmly reassuring one, against which colours and shapes can be appreciated to their full potential. But rampantly floral fabrics and china; bright dragged, stippled or stencilled walls; Persian and rag rugs; earthy striped dhurries and kilims; and the ubiquitous dresser proudly displaying the colourful bounty of decades of car-boot sales and thrift-shop browsing offer an overflowing cornucopia of colour and pattern, a jubilant celebration of village life.

Nor need a country look be worthy. Natural materials do not preclude wit, opulence or occasional forays into frivolity. If you have a mind to make a twinkling chandelier from bottle tops, go for it.

The experience of working on a magazine, building and dismantling sets for photography, demonstrates what an ephemeral art decoration is, and that having decided on an absolute rule, it is often inspiring to go ahead and break it. Much consists in trying a swathe of this, a tassel of that, keeping the colours either all clean or all muddy and taking the main elements from a narrow wedge of the spectrum, using contrasts of colour and texture as condiments. Attractive accessories – pots, bowls and cushions – shown off against sympathetic backgrounds make a huge difference. Walls can be painted and repainted in a matter of minutes. Above all, set out to lose the anxiety of seeing decoration as a life-or-death matter. Making a pleasantly countrified context for your life consists in doing what comes naturally. And enjoying it.

CHAPTER ONE

ENTRANCES & HALLWAYS

BECKONING ENTRANCE

Everything that is best about the country can be found here — open doors, a glimpse of an overflowing, sunny garden and a sense of welcome. The much-trodden path and a bright yellow front door give a friendly overlay to the eighteenth-century symmetry of this English country house. Nature contributes generously to the appeal of the house in the form of a shaggy black grape vine that curtains the upper windows, and exuberant purple clematis that flanks the door, softening the formality.

ENTRANCES &
HALLWAYS

The front door of a house should signify welcome. The garden gate, the path and the door itself, are the first things a visitor sees, and often suggest something of the character of the owner. If a gate, its paint distressed beyond endurance, collapses in a heap of splintered timber, or a path becomes perilous because of patches of lethal moss, and the door displays a *chiaroscuro* of ancient dust upon its mouldings, your visitors may advance with trepidation. Or, worse still, they may retreat in panic as the first spider falls down the back of their necks, and fail to deliver the competition prize or the unexpected marriage proposal.

It is surprisingly easy to overlook your front door when decorating indoors, yet the approach to a house leaves an enduring image, and first impressions tend to colour everything that follows. There is something distinctly appealing about a gate that opens without involving engineering; the absence of a certain kind of dog – loud, malevolent or merely over-interested; a neat front path, preferably of old brick, leading without demur to a refined porch. For most of us this is a fantasy, but even if details differ, some general principles still apply.

The first rule is to take a good critical look at other people's solutions and plagiarize ruthlessly. The most obvious advice is to enhance the original character of your home. Ancient cottages built piecemeal over the centuries, together with stolid late nineteenth- and early twentieth-century architecture can bear a number of approaches.

If you are fortunate to own a perfect symmetrical Georgian rectory, an elegant clapboard house or a simple stone *manoir*, you would be wise to echo its formal simplicity in the way you treat the external details such as paths and porches, gates and door furniture. Ideally the materials you use should be the best you can afford – 'quick fixes' may occasionally be the appropriate response to a hybrid cottage of vague descendancy, but the cool perfectionist logic of Georgian or Shaker architecture draws immediate attention to any imposed details that are of the wrong period or of tacky construction.

PRESERVING FRONT DOORS

The perfect front door is one that is sheltered from the worst of the weather by a porch or entrance overhang. It should be illuminated after dark and an appropriately antique bell or knocker attached; something that functions and does not induce a sense of anxious uncertainty about whether or not the ring at the door has been heard. Pots of lemon verbena or lilies outside a main door breathe a fragrant welcome, while scented climbers and a seat are thoughtful additions. But greenery has a way of proving unruly if not kept firmly pruned. Your front garden, if tended and nurtured, may be the ideal place from which to survey the world and indulge in good old-fashioned neighbourly gossip; the sort of pastime that lowers blood pressure and lessens stress levels.

It is worth carrying out almost any kind of remedial work to preserve an original front door, since nothing ruins a facade more effectively than an inappropriate door. If you have to replace it, study neighbouring houses of the same vintage and find the heaviest similar door you can that has the correct sort of mouldings and panels. Many older houses have glazed top panels, and etched or stained glass looks wonderful with the late afternoon sunlight falling through it. Letterboxes and knockers should not be skimpy, badly placed or contain any trace of brushed aluminium or plastic. Good solid antiques made from brass or painted cast iron are affordable, easy to come by, and give an air of authenticity to a door, however new. Matching numerals are desirable, or you might commission a stained-glass fanlight panel.

MAKING AN ENTRANCE

It is a sad fact that entrance halls are magnets for clutter. They breed canine paraphernalia and muddy shoes, elderly tennis racquets and bicycle bits. Not only is your hall the first visible sight of the interior,

ALL-PURPOSE HALL
The spacious entrance hall to an eighteenth-century home has evolved to become the family sitting room where tennis racquets and walking sticks overflow from a Chinese vase. In summer, the handsome front door is open in welcome, and in winter a fire greets the chilly visitor.

but it is also the filter which collects all the school bags, old sports socks and outdoor debris blown in with the visitor. No matter what cunning storage system you counter this with, there is something innately subversive about umbrellas and wet boots which allows them to congregate in a muddled heap. The best approach is to weatherproof your hall as much as possible with high doormats, indestructible flagstones and a generous expanse of coat-hooks. If there is space, a hall table is essential, but will require the same regular and rigorous editing as the contents of the average handbag.

A seductive hall is something to aspire to in the country, where mud and dirt must be prevented from penetrating the house. The first priorities when decorating are usually the kitchen and the living room, followed by the bedrooms and bathroom. A hall comes way down the line, once the other rooms have been coerced into civilization. Only then, and for those of us wedged between jobs and children, that time may never come, can one indulge the luxurious impulse to place a posy on the table, some pot pourri in a blue Chinese bowl on the radiator shelf, or a sparkling Bohemian mirror on the wall.

HALL FLOORING

It is important to make the right initial and unavoidable decisions about flooring. One of the irritations of life is that you tend to get what you pay for, and it often shows. Cheap haircord carpet will develop bald patches wherever adolescent feet care to tramp, and may produce wild tufts of aberrant wool where your cat has determined to dig its way into the living room. Most shiny bare wood, with or without slithering rugs, can give the impression of a slippery, chill atmosphere, though good warm lighting, the most essential attribute of an inviting hall, may counteract this. Lacquers and varnishes impart an unsympathetic hardness to wooden floors, while the hard labour of applying beeswax polish with hours of elbow grease gives an unsurpassable finish.

Alternatively, a scrubbed or limed wooden floor – only for less than magnificent boards - has an appealing cottagey quality; and painted boards in quiet, muted Shaker colours make a flattering frame to toning

IN THE
GRAND MANOR
Not everyone can aspire to a rotunda which sheds light upon their stairwell. This Georgian house in Somerset, England, has been lovingly restored by its owner, down to the last variation of traditional ridged and barley sugar spindles on the stairs. Stencilled Etruscan urns on a lively colourwashed wall are a witty reference to the aspirations of the original architect and are quite at home with an eighteenth-century medallion quilt.

WARM WELCOME

*Carefully chosen muted
colours make this hall an
inviting place. Ancient
timber beams and a
pleasantly battered door with
appropriate hinges and latch
give an antique authenticity;
powdery terracotta tiles
marry peacefully with the
walls and a handsome
painted dresser whose
surprising yellow side may be
an unintended relic of the
past, adds just the right flash
of brightness. The clock, the
naive painting and the
striped cushions are chosen
with a subtle eye to
harmonize with the rest of
the surroundings.*

A ROVER'S RETROSPECTIVE

The owner of this nineteenth-century cottage is a traveller and a distinguished authority on tribal textiles - a passion clearly visible in the hall, which was once the kitchen, that leads to a tall narrow staircase. The shades of kindly natural green on Lloyd loom chair, doors and risers make a perfect foil for the brilliant kaleidoscope of an Indian wedding canopy, a Shahsavani kilim from Northern Iran and a Jain appliqué wallhanging.

rugs. Natural wood has an intractable browness which seems almost to absorb light, so the most successful country interiors temper any prevailing woodiness with carefully placed splashes of bold colour. Advocates of the natural look should bear in mind the depressing fact that nothing advertises its cost and quality quite so prominently as the unadorned raw material: broad planks of oak, a chequerboard of stone or naturally aged terracotta, all look terrific and will probably bankrupt you. However, your grandchildren will be grateful for the legacy.

The demolition of old buildings can yield wonderful bounty to an opportunist decorator armed with a large vehicle and a ready supply of cash. Before you stack your car with a battered pile of hardwood parquet though, consider the number of hours involved in removing the previous, undesirable finish. Can you really bear to live without a floor for the time needed to strip sticky black varnish from every piece? Architectural salvage yards are also good hunting grounds for old floors, though it is worth checking the price, since dealers have been

ONE HORSEPOWER

A spare and elegant hall, its stone flags warmed by an autumnal kilim and its severity leavened by reminders of childhood, is given a sumptuous touch by curtains pelmeted in gold. Beyond, a room with a chequered floor and walls of glowing currant red beckons.

SUBTLE
SPLENDOUR
The mutable Gustavian blue-grey-green of this hall was inspired by an old, weathered piece of cast-iron railing. Among the blues, this is a colour that has a natural warmth and a strong component of yellow which allies well with the untreated wood of the floor, the surprising pink of the skirting board and the blots of quiet colour cast by a magnificent Gothick stained-glass door.

known to sell old floors for quite a bit more than the cost of new ones, and there are ways of treating new softwood floors to make them look as if several armies have used them as parade grounds.

Suitable and indestructible floors for halls are warm, worn bricks or quarry tiles; encaustic tiles and slate and granite flagstones, which are splendidly handsome, if a little chill underfoot. More affordable options include linoleum, which can be cleaned with paraffin, and which has an old-fashioned warmth about it; polished concrete paving slabs in carefully chosen colours; and tough seagrass, sisal and coir matting.

FLOOR COVERINGS

Having made your most expensive investment, you can proceed to the enjoyable task of embellishing the floor with two or three antique Persian rugs in stained-glass colours. Kilims can be found in every combination of colour. The earthy spectrum produced by natural dyes always looks good, and ages gently. Your hall is not the place for

WINDING STAIR
A clever piece of home-building, in the form of a curved brick stairway, leads from the kitchen of this eighteenth-century farmhouse in the Black mountains, Wales. Terracotta floor, jade green table cover and cornflower blue walls suggest Matisse, rather than moorland.

25

UNABASHED DAZZLE

The owners of this cottage import tiles from all over the world, and the floors and walls bear testament to a fascination with pattern. The parrot-strewn diamond motifs in the cloakroom were plagiarized from a sixteenth-century Florentine house — a bold and carefree experiment in a tiny room that succeeds triumphantly. This is a great tribute to the power of the notebook. Always carry a sketchbook or camera around with you to record your decorative ideas. It is never easy to remember clearly exact details, yet here it is the precise balance of highly textured and unexpected colour that works so well. Outside, the hall is flooded with light and is given warmth by unadorned wood and terracotta.

A DIP INTO HISTORY

The heart of this Yorkshire priory is a huge thirteenth-century hall. The present owners have brought the house to life with hand-tinted distemper on the walls which looks like time-weathered plaster, worn paving slabs on the floors and a rich mixture of textures and textiles, ethnic and local. These elements are punctuated by traditional American stencil designs and delicate motifs copied from fabrics. The recently added porch looks as if it has been there forever.

HOMAGE TO WOOD

This heavily beamed house dates from 1500, and is furnished wherever possible with pieces from the period, selected with the help of an expert in early English furniture. The abundance of glowing waxed oak gives a warmth which is enhanced by tapestry and velvet, kilims and middle Eastern rugs. The vast dog, dwarfing door and seat might well have strayed in after a medieval jousting match.

RIGHT

PALE AND INTERESTING

A distinctly Gothick entrance hall, this area contains a carved chair; an impressive turned wooden pole bearing ancient curtains bordered with Art Nouveau lilies; and a theatrical looking door with massively curlicued hinges. Sensible, dirt-repellant coir matting on the floor gives a casual warmth, and the conglomeration of walking sticks, umbrellas, baseball bats, tennis racquets and lacrosse sticks suggests a family prepared for anything.

LEFT

THE COLOUR WHITE

Utter simplicity and many shades of white show the few elegant elements of this modern hallway in their stark perfection. The vagaries of light have a dramatic part to play: the spiral staircase becomes quite ethereal, bleached out by the window behind, while the ceramic cheese drainers are given graphic definition by shadows, and a humble, crocheted shopping bag takes on a crisp, sculptural texture.

anything precious. Needlepoint, oriental, and Bessarabian rugs are fragile and will not thrive under the uncaring tramp of feet.

USING COLOUR

Two things make a country hallway come alive; colour and light. Colour is an unpredictable pleasure to play with. It usually does not produce quite the effect you were expecting, but if you can hang on to your courage and an open mind, the hall is a good place in which to experiment. Rich, strong, glowing colours which might be overwhelming as an environment in which to pass much time, are wonderfully dramatic backgrounds for a transitory hallway.

Your hall should be a blank canvas on which to be daring. This is the place to try out the warm partnership of a terracotta colourwash with the soft scumbled colour of old stone, or to flood with raw Mediterranean sunshine, using the yellow ochre and Prussian blue suggested by your chosen kilim. An element of warmth is essential, as no-one likes a cold hall. If the colours seem too heavy at first, live with

RIGHT

BARE MAGNIFICENCE

Acres of polished black and white marble, Ionic pilasters, a sinuous staircase and delicate plasterwork motifs signal the best of Irish Georgian architecture. Non-palace owners might care to emulate the spare perfection of the decor, or investigate plaster casts for comparable crisp details with which to enliven bare walls.

the effect for a while, adding touches of sparkle with bevelled mirrors and paintings on the walls, or flowers, pebbles and driftwood on the table. Interiors that bring a surge of pleasure to the heart often do so by virtue of a brave use of colour.

Take your colour cue from the possessions you have, or if you are starting from scratch, have a good look at your favourite paintings, textiles or interiors in museums, books and magazines. Ponder the impact that your preferred colours would have on your walls. Often the most irresistible paintings or fabrics are not composed of flat colour; their richness comes from innumerable strokes or threads of close, but not identical shades. This makes for a liveliness that you can emulate very easily with paint and brush.

CHOOSING PAINT

When it come to colour, the world divides roughly into two kinds of people: those who thrill to the kitsch bravado and exuberant colours of Mexico and the Mediterranean; and those who feel more at home with the cool restraint and natural materials of the Shakers and the Scandinavians. There is safety and calm in the organic-looking blues, greens and russets beloved of the Northerners, and their favourite soft colours create effortless harmonies.

Most natural country interiors look best with warm, rather than brilliant white walls. When displaying objects in halls, aim for an uncluttered paucity of beautiful objects. This is where a somewhat Oriental still-life of flotsam collected on a winter seashore walk looks particularly good. And prepare to get busy with the beeswax. If you yearn for pale polished wood, plaited rag rugs and tongued-and-grooved panels painted Wedgwood grey-blue, you must be aware that every speck of dust will proclaim itself.

Gloss paint for wood is neat, tidy and practical, and has become an ingrained and unquestioned habit. However there are more interesting colours and textures available which have the same hardiness as gloss. Shaker paints are one example. They are available in eight colours and dry to a tough matt finish, which can be easily sanded back.

BUDGET GRANDEUR
The sunfilled hallway of this nineteenth-century Quaker meeting house is an exercise in tasteful fakery — the panelled walls and dado were concocted from medium-density fibreboard in the original style of the house. On close inspection the detail is superb. Quarry tiles were laid on the diagonal on top of a timber floor — it should not have worked but it does. According to the owner: 'Not having any money is a very good formula for decorating, because you can't afford to make mistakes.'

GILDING & USING GOLD LEAF

There is something irrationally seductive about Gold. Its historical associations date from Tutankhamen via the Three Wise Men, illuminated manuscripts and alchemy, while today gold is visible in the trappings of royalty and in just about every wedding ring that is made. Gold is seen as noble, pure and unchanging, providing a standard by which lesser metals are found wanting. It has warmth, and reflects light with a lively glow. Figuratively and literally, gold is richness.

Fortunately, you do not need to be Midas to bask in gilded splendour at home. You can indulge a passion for gold by creating gilded objects using cobweb fine gold leaf (or its more affordable cousin, Dutch metal) and a little skill – the glorious results are out of all proportion to the small expenditure you will have to make.

Although professional gilders spend much of their youth learning the intricacies of using gesso and glue, for those of us to whom absolute perfection of finish is neither essential nor desirable, the technique of transfer-leaf gilding is much easier to perfect and the end result gleams just as extravagantly.

Once you have mastered the basic techniques of gilding, you will find that it is the perfect embellishment for mouldings, lamps, mirror and picture frames, plaster obelisks, wooden caskets and letter racks. After a heady gold-rush on your part, your hall will extend a subtly luxurious welcome to friends. You may find that you cannot stop here. The possibilities are endless and you could find yourself compelled to bring glamour to the kitchen with gilded trays and tea-caddies, add opulence to wine and candlelight with gold stars stamped on dining room walls and curtains, and to transform a collection of everyday objects from the spartan into the sumptuous. Decorative techniques such as oil-gilding, parcel gilding and antiquing are perfect for this magical operation which is simple to achieve yet hugely effective.

DARKLY GLEAMING
DETAILS
A sumptuous still-life of gilded plaster gives a hint of the range and subtlety possible with Dutch gold leaf and antique finishes. Gold is a wonderful punctuation and a little goes a long way. Pristine gilded urns and acanthus leaves may be further embellished by a touch of Fuller's earth, umber paint, boot polish or antiquing varnish.

OIL GILDING

Dutch metal leaf is thicker than other leafs and only comes in press-down transfer form. Loose silver leaf tarnishes and so needs varnishing. Loose gold-leaf is the water-gilder's medium; exorbitant and delicate. Pure gold transfer-leaf needs no varnishing and behaves like transfer Dutch metal.

OIL-GILDING

This simply involves applying a layer of special quick-drying varnish called goldsize over the surface to be gilded. When almost completely dry, between one and five hours after application, transfer-leaf, mounted on tissue paper, is pressed on to the size and the tissue peeled away. The drier the size, the brighter the gilt (see left).

PARCEL GILT

The term parcel gilt comes from the old English for 'part or portion', and means just that: only the most visible parts, the highlights of the surface, are covered with leaf, and the rest is given a gilt look with cheaper bronzing powders (finely ground alloys of brass, copper and tin). These, together with oils and resins, make up commercial gold paint, which has a disappointingly dull and gritty finish. Decorators prefer to 'pounce' or dust the powders on to a film of tacky varnish, usually goldsize, and then brush off the excess to reveal a finish of almost liquid smoothness and glow.

With any gilt finish, the traditional colours for the underpainting are dark red oxide (the colour of the smooth clay bole used by water-gilders) or yellows, varying from the lemon used for leafwork on wrought-iron gates, to the yellow ochre car spray paint used here (yellow is good at masking flaws).

OIL-GILDED PICTURE MOULDING

An eighteenthth-century picture moulding has been oil-gilded with water-gilded highlights and its recesses pounced with bronzing powder.

POUNCING

Apply an even coat of goldsize to your object and when tacky, dust on the powder. Wear a mask for this. Wait at least eight hours until the goldsize is thoroughly hard before applying a second layer to take the leaf. But this time only varnish the lighlights, where the leaf will sit. Wait patiently until the size is almost dry and you can press its surface without leaving a fingerprint, then lay the transfer-leaf, cutting it into manageable strips and pressing gently so that it comes away from the tissue backing. Gently brush away the excess and a few hours later polish your object lightly with a piece of cotton wool to obtain a good finish.

ANTIQUING AN URN

This plastic 'Regency' urn has been given a 100 per cent leaf treatment to deliberately exploit the way that laid leaf will crack and split when pressed into relief. The background colour is red oxide car spray paint, producing a perfectly smooth ground. Brush on the coat of goldsize, again waiting until it is dry to the touch before pressing on the leaf, at the same time controlling the amount of red showing through by passing over the surface with more scraps of the transfer gold. Dust off before antiquing.

To protect the underlying goldsize, use very dilute French enamel varnish.

REGENCY URN

To finish off the urn, French enamel varnishes are washed and splattered for differing effects: brown for patina, vermilion for richness.

POUNCING

Pounce with bronzing powders to give an extraordinary effect of ageing. Always remember to varnish bronzing powders, and Dutch metal, to prevent tarnishing.

LIVING ROOMS
& PARLOURS

LIVING ROOMS
& PARLOURS

*S*ummer or winter, the perfect place for reading the Sunday
papers, whether sprawled in the sunshine by open French
doors or snacking on toasted muffins in front of a warming
fire, is the living room. It should be a welcoming refuge from
the serious business of life.

The room itself is a comparatively modern invention. It was, at first,
a luxury confined to the rich and leisured classes – more humble types
had to make do with a corner of the kitchen, except in those parts of
the world where the sun shines dependably and the yard, garden or
verandah took on the air of a relaxed outdoor room. Where rain and
chill dominate however, the great indoors rules. Everyone, particularly
anyone with children, shares a great collective sigh of relief as summer
approaches and life can be lived in the open air. Many a furrowed
parental brow has been smoothed by the great exhilaration of no longer
having to worry about crumbs and cola becoming engrained in the
carpet. With summer comes the knowledge that the appalling excess
energy of the average child and their accompanying riotous games, not
to mention lengthy experiments with paper and glue, need not take
place among the Bohemian glass and Regency whatnots, the treasured
objects of the living room.

This is not to assume that the whole world strains to maintain
civilization in the face of juvenile subversion. However, there is
something serene and peaceful about the summer exodus to the garden
and the feeling of relief at not having to worry about the paintwork or
the rare and precious Aubusson rug. If you do happen to share your
home with children, or dogs, there are different practical criteria for a
successful interior from those that operate after offspring. With
children around, rickety tables, particularly those covered with
breakable objects, will collapse; pale carpets will exercise a magnetic

CANINE COMFORT

*The essential ingredients for
the classic country house are
all here – a battered leather
sofa, gloomy paintings of
rural life, and an outrageous,
badly-behaved dog.
P G Wodehouse would have
felt quite at home here.*

attraction for tomato ketchup; precious marquetry will have to suffer the indignities of hot cups and wet glasses; lacquer bowls will be used as ashtrays; fitted upholstery will wear and rip beneath the relentless onslaught of boot-clad feet – whatever house rules you try to maintain, these things and worse will happen, so temper your ideas accordingly.

CREATING A FAMILY ROOM

The living room tends to be the place where familial civil wars occur – you can hardly ban your children from sharing it, but nor can you then expect it to be a quiet, uncluttered haven in which to entertain your revered and ancient relatives. If you can run to a separate, indestructible room with its own television, solely for the use of people from the building block phase to that of illicit cigarettes, you will be able to ignore the entire problem. Otherwise the trick is to make the living room comfortable and communal, displaying a prevalence of washable fabrics, your really precious possessions out of reach, and a simple sense of style – the fewer rules you have to fret about, the happier everyone will be.

FLOORING SOLUTIONS

The floor finish represents the biggest and most irreversible outlay, and will dictate the way that the room is used and the colours that will work in it, so it is worth giving it a little thought. Since most normal children like nothing better than sitting on the floor sprinkling bits of food over a wide area, you would be wise not to invest in a vast area of cream thick-pile carpet until your children have left home. On the other hand, there is much to be said for treating the floor as a large piece of wooden furniture on which to sit, lay or read.

Fitted carpet maximizes space magically, is warm and comforting, but somehow does not quite have a country flavour. Also, it shows every crumb and wine spill unless you use such a jazzy design that everyone automatically assumes you dust it with cake and drench it with claret whenever you get the chance. Dirt-repelling treatments are only partially successful, since they quickly lose their effectiveness in

CARIBBEAN
BRIGHT
Complementary blue and yellow with a dash of bright orange are not the colours one expects in the staid backwaters of rural England. But striped with sunlight, or heated by a giant French woodburning stove, this is an interior to energize the spirit and cheer the heart.

areas of heavy traffic.

Sisal, coconut, coir and seagrass matting are all economical and highly countrified, but their visually attractive texture can be uncomfortably abrasive to the foot or seat. Rush matting has the same rugged appeal, is similarly well-behaved and kinder to the skin. It can be laid loose on a wood or tile floor and dust or dirt will percolate through, to be easily dealt with by a quick vacuum. Dry air makes matting brittle, and a judicious watering is in order when a heatwave has baked the garden brown. They all have a wonderful capacity to shrug off the daily accumulation of domestic detritus.

RUGS FOR LIVING ROOMS

The perfect compromise between grace and comfort is a scattering of rugs on stained, polished or painted wood. The dilemma here – apart from the easily solved problems of slippery floor surfaces – is one of choice. The whole world has conspired to give you myriad rugs as rich and subtle as the painter Tissot's palette. You can exploit this Aladdin's cave by using several different rugs in a family of colours – North African desert Berbers, North American Navajo flat-weave, Indian dhurries, faded Aubusson, African Afghan kelims – as long as the colours marry well, the different weaves and designs simply add Baroque richness to an interior.

FLOORBOARD TREATMENTS

Shiny new floorboards and great unbroken expanses of plywood lack character, and while you may not wish to distress them with hammers and chisels or age them with treacly antiquing varnish, you might like to give them a bit more life by painting them, staining them with a clear finish that lets the grain show, or by applying a stencilled design. If you decide to paint or stencil, it is a good idea to look at traditional American reference sources for inspiration. The itinerant decorators of the eighteenth and nineteenth century were the absolute masters of the painted floor and floorcloth. Generally, the simpler the design the better – big diamonds with a plain border, for instance, are handsome

PAINTERLY CHARM
A motley dazzle of clashing colour bedecks this painter's house. It is furnished with charming, locally bought old objects such as rag rugs, milliners' dummies and jewel-bright quilts. The Turkish-inspired cupboard was painted by the owner to echo the dominant colours of the living room.

and do not date. Interesting, variable and slightly transparent colour looks good, possibly aged with an umber glaze and finished with many coats of protective varnish or polish. Polish gives a more sympathetic finish to painted furniture, but floors need to be rather more hard wearing, so polyurethane varnish may be in order.

LIVING COLOUR

Solid bright gloss colour, wherever it is used, is anathema to an authentic country look. Its great crime is to be boring – colour should be lively and age interestingly, and gloss paint just isn't, and doesn't. Better to use humble emulsion paint to impart a subtle veil of colour to a wooden floor that has a slightly open grain. It can be painted on, wiped off, and given intensity with polish; one of the new and ecologically sound water-based varnishes; or polyurethane varnish.

Broken paint techniques are useful for enlivening a floor finish: 'floating marble' made with oil colour and equal amounts of oil glaze and white spirit painted on to a coloured ground; spattering, combing, colourwashing and sponging are all feasible over a large area, and all invite harmonizing experiment with paint finishes on skirting, doors and other woodwork.

PAINT FINISHES

Even plain paint has changed recently. Instead of gloss which used to be the only choice for wood, there are now various ranges of casein-based paint, made by traditional methods, which have the matt bloom of suede, give a rich and symphonic colour, and are wonderfully versatile. They can be thinned to make a translucent wash on bare wood, used undiluted for strong matt colour, smoothed to a durable sheen with wire wool or sanded back to give a look of colonial antiquity. For smaller objects and furniture there are new water-based scumbles and crackle glazes that are easy to use and less damaging to the environment than their old-fashioned solvent-based equivalents. Their disadvantage is that they dry quickly and are therefore troublesome over large areas where you need to keep a wet edge.

RUS IN URBE
A magnificent pair of curtains adorn the living room of a countrified town house which belongs to two designers: the misleading forest framed by the window is, in fact, a London square. The generous swags and tassels of the checked silk curtains are echoed in the stencilled frieze around the wall, which is the work of an itinerant American folk artist.

PREVIOUS PAGE

PAINTINGS AND
PERSIAN RUGS

*A traditional parlour boasts
a lively painting of Daphne
and Apollo by the owner,
resplendent in a frame which
was a gift from a local junk
dealer. The duck-egg blue
walls were a successful first
experiment in rag-rolling,
and the Turkish and Persian
rugs add a rosy air.*

Colour can work magic. Nothing else can effect a total
transformation in a room so quickly or easily. While a passion for
unadulterated bare polished wood, white walls and terracotta tiles is a
classic response to country living, there is another school of thought
which counters grey skies and bare, dripping branches with all the
joyful brilliance of Gauguin's paintings of Tahiti, or vivid Mediterranean hues. These days, mass-produced paint is a pure pleasure to
use. Forget the anxieties of slow-drying primers, sanding, filling, drips,
runs and endless waiting, only to find obstinate sticky bits that leave
indelible streaks on floor and clothes. This new generation of antique
paint behaves faultlessly and unlike gloss, is sympathetic to wood.
Stripped pine still holds its own, but why live with treacle when you

could create a rainbow? Ignore all this if brown is your favourite colour, but maybe the courageous boldness of some of these bright interiors makes your heart beat a little faster, and will encourage you to rifle through the paint swatches in your local home decorating store. As the practical Homework project shows (see pages 58-63), you can work vibrant, sophisticated miracles using ordinary emulsion paint and a dash of panache.

STENCILLING IDEAS

Stencils are the easy way to embellish walls and furniture. They were once the only form of wall decoration until wallpaper became the affordable and fashionable alternative in the nineteenth century. But stencils vary. Bought ready-cut stencils are fine for the faint-hearted, and, for architectural pastiches, an element of crisp right angles and perfectly curvilinear swags may be appropriate. But best of all is the enjoyment to be had from designing and cutting your own stencils, using a motif which means something to you. The essence of an authentic country look is not perfection, but character, quirkiness and even the odd mistake. You do not need to be a creative genius: books containing drawings of out-of-copyright images are an unsurpassed hunting ground for motifs which you can enlarge and combine as you please. The only tools you need are a scalpel (never ever forget that surgeons use them for operations – they can be lethal, and need to be used cautiously and kept away from children) and acetate. Plastic document folders are ideal: easy to come by, they have a useful static cling which helps them stay in place while you sponge or stipple your design on wall, table or lampshade. For a start, it is usually a mistake to stencil straight onto flat paint – the result is often crude and accentuates the mechanical aspect of the craft. Better to enrich surfaces which are already lively with depths and textures of interesting layers of colour. With quick-drying water-based or acrylic paints, you can leave the stencil in place (held with low-tack masking tape) while you add subtle highlights or shading, or a nuance of different colour.

Coordination not cacophony is what you are aiming for – friends and

LEFT

COTTAGE
SIMPLICITY
The most basic ingredients –
old floor pamments, grizzled
plank doors, a red and
indigo kilim, a cast iron
stove and soft terracotta walls
– create an interior that is
timeless and inviting.

family will mutter darkly behind your back if there is no coherent masterplan. You may, for example, be in love with yellow, and you might also be lucky enough to have a huge paisley throw with which to glorify your sofa. To put the two together to their mutual advantage, you could colourwash your walls with toning layers of buttercup and saffron, and stencil a frieze of umber and cinnamon paisley motifs around the walls. Having succeeded with that, you could echo the paisley with stencilled lampshades. A plain MDF (medium-density fibreboard) coffee table can become a thing of beauty with the addition of a raw umber and burnt sienna glaze, stencilled with your paisleys in russet and foxy reds, and finished with a discreet touch of gold lining. This might make you turn back to your lampshades to give them a gold edge top and bottom. Add tasselled Ikat cushions from the same palette, a circular table with a faded red and brown patchwork quilt and generous curtains in rich madras checks lined with calico. You will end up with a room that will beam when the sun is shining and surround you with warmth when the nights are long.

As long as you confine your colours to a small and harmonizing wedge of the spectrum for most of the major areas, you can then use small areas of contrast and counterpoint as punctuation – scarlet lacquer boxes, brass lampstands, a dark green marbled fire surround, a verdigris mirror frame or découpage roses on a black painted screen.

LIGHTING FOR LIVING ROOMS

Lighting is one of the most important aspects of interior decoration, and one of the least considered. Keep lots of candles to hand for special occasions. Pools of light distributed around the room make it look intimate and inviting, particularly when accompanied by the radiant flicker of firelight – it is almost worth turning the central heating off to indulge in the unbeatable luxury of an open fire, even if gas, rather than pinewood, is your fuel. At all costs avoid using anything to shed unkind light from the middle of the ceiling. Spotlights always look utilitarian and are out of place in a room whose purpose is to ease away the cares of the day. Unless *petit point* needlepoint is a major consideration in your

THEATRICAL
FLOUNCES
The owner of this house is a film set dresser, and her splendidly swagged curtains, with their fringes and rosettes, are pure theatre. They even made a brief appearance in The French Lieutenant's Woman. *There is further nostalgia in the fleet of family photos and the elderly furniture. The ensemble exudes comfort and humanity, and the autumn leaf colours are a triumph of visual harmony.*

RIGHT

PLAIN AUTHENTIC

This cottage has been lovingly restored: new windows in the parlour were carved from blocks of local sandstone, and the traditional high-backed elm window seat was copied from the original. A slate-lined cupboard houses sturdy earthenware.

ANCIENT LIGHT

*The massive Norman walls of
one of the oldest
continuously inhabited
houses in Britain are
blanched by tentative shafts
of summer sunlight.
Handstitched hexagonal
patchwork draped casually on
the arm of a huge sofa adds
a touch of colour to an
otherwise spartan room.*

life and you need powerful lighting, an assortment of table lamps will provide enough illumination. Lighting is cheap and easy, and many different light sources give a room life.

FURNISHING WITH TEXTILES

Textiles enter into the same category of cheap, easy and portable furnishings. It is no coincidence that nomadic tribes – the Berbers and the Kurds among them – are pre-eminent weavers. Textiles make instant homes anywhere. You can hang them on the wall, throw them on the floor, drape them on the seating or swag them at the window. Heavy and quilted for warmth, or floating and airy to drift in a summer breeze, they soften hard edges, contribute warmth and texture, and there are many permutations of pattern and colour to explore.

The most important rule with textiles is generosity. Curtains for large windows require a daunting amount of fabric to look good. It is always better to have plenty of something cheap than too little of something precious. If rose-strewn chintz is prohibitively expensive, it can still be enjoyed in small quantities as cushions, pelmets or as a border for more affordable plain-dyed fabric.

Textile wholesalers are worth investigating. Indian sari shops sell irresistible silks and muslins for ludicrously small sums, and calico is cheap and stylish. Tassels and borders, braid, fringing and gimp are useful for adding glamour to an economical window treatment, while lining or quilting lightweight fabrics gives them substance.

SIMPLE STYLE

At the other extreme, Shaker interiors did without frills and furbelows altogether, and while they could not be called cosy, they certainly had a grace and serenity that is good for the spirit. Prints are out of place for Shaker-inspired rooms since they relied on woven checks or stripes for decoration, but while authenticity is laudable, it is not obligatory. It is a question of mood rather than edict – for some reason spotless rooms, empty but for a polished wooden rocking chair and an oval box on a table, make printed fabrics look frivolous.

HOMAGE TO A GREAT SCULPTOR
Elizabeth Frink lived in this converted stable block in Dorset, England. The huge, galleried main room served a multiplicity of functions and is now wonderfully enriched by her handsome and appropriate horses. Everything in the room is simple and good, with touches of Prussian blue providing a rich contrast to the prevailing Persian carpet colours. Space and light dominate, the room is airy without being chill or intimidating, and the atmosphere expresses the generous humanity of its talented creator.

The Shaker ethos was not mean, but it was spartan. Plainness was a virtue to aspire to, and amid the complexities of twentieth-century life, simplicity still brings calm and solace. Perversely, this is a way of life and a style of furnishing that is difficult to achieve because you cannot cheat. It is a look based on perfection, which is a rare commodity. You cannot fudge a Shaker dresser – it has to have exact dovetails; you cannot even fake a Shaker floorboard – the smooth shine is the patina of years of sweeping and polishing. But you can create a satisfactory pastiche that is a little easier to live with, using good basic materials that are cared for and unadorned in sober colonial colours, with shutters rather than the ephemera of curtains, an oval plaited rag rug and an absence of clutter.

Unadorned wood is the main feature of Scandinavian interiors too, and Mediterranean houses are often bare but for hard, functional furniture and terracotta tiles. It is a spacious, airy way of living, in perfect harmony with summer. Its brisk severity can be mitigated to cope with winter by the addition of a glowing stove, heavy rugs and thick curtains. Stacks of cushions can give the softness essential for winter comfort – it is unthinkable to spend the winter sitting in a wooden chair without a buffer of feathers and down.

CHOOSING FURNITURE

Country furniture tends to be of the solid, comfortable and unpretentious variety. Huge squashy sofas in chintz or checks, armchairs to curl up in, all-purpose painted chests for storage and which double as tables or window-seats and masses of shelves spilling books are the sort of things that have an affinity with a view of distant hills and cattle.

Adequate storage is essential. Most people at the back of their minds aspire to the perfectly ordered world in which, like the Shakers, they could find anything in a moment, even in a power cut. A generous excess of storage space is the way to achieve this dream, and to value and nurture your possessions. Ordered and considered presentation is what distinguishes a precious collection from a chaos of clutter.

SATURATED COLOUR

A bright crescendo of sunny colour in a corner of Tricia Guild's living room is provided by a collection of favourite objects atop a Biedermeier sewing table: Italian glass fruit, a vase by Ivor Moseley and ceramics by Liz Hodges are flanked by a bold Howard Hodgkin splashy sofa. Her advice is to make a basic colourboard from sizeable swatches of fabric and samples of paint viewed in natural and artificial light, to echo and play on the main theme in the details, and to trust your instincts.

PAINT EFFECTS

Nothing gives so much for so little as a dash of paint. Once you have taken the first courageous step away from the safety of matt magnolia paint and have discovered the magical transformation that a subtle colourwash can bestow to your walls and your spirits, you will never again fall victim to the meretricious appeal of 'hint of pink.'

Rooms that most often inspire eager plagiarism have one thing in common – colour. This is not to dismiss the monastic charm of white walls and simple furniture – the perfect country classic. But there is a huge, exciting repertoire of colour to be explored, whether bright or subtle, Mediterranean warm or Northern cool, matt or polished, smooth or textured. Life is too short not to seize innocent life-enhancing pleasures where we may.

For decades, the big paint manufacturers have monopolized our walls with their choice of paint types: silk, matt, gloss and not much else. They are serviceable, but somehow less than inspiring. Even their myriad colours in huge swatches never seem to have the intensity, radiance or glow that make you rush for your paintbrush. Far more interesting are the new paints made by small specialist firms, based on traditional materials and pigments – bright chalky colours imported from Turkey, rich ochres and umbers concocted from ground earth and the muted, slightly off-colours researched from historic houses.

There is more to paint than meets the eye. Different ingredients give depth and bloom – lead-based paints, wicked and dangerous though they may be, have a quality and texture that cannot be emulated by vinyl. Gloss paint is the worst atrocity in the modern paint pantheon and has no sympathy with anything – it is noxious to apply, ages ungracefully and is lethal to remove. Painting should be fun, after all.

The obsession with sanding down and preparing well has obscured the point of it all, which is to have a good time and to create a unique

FOUND
INSPIRATION
Sometimes research will provide you with a ready-made decorative image. The Florentine capital, left, was photocopied from a design book and enlarged to provide a repeat at cornice height.

The wall was first colourwashed using unthinned distemper tinted with yellow ochre and heavily brushed out. The photocopies were gummed to the wall with wallpaper paste then tinted with a smear of the same paint to subdue their harshness. A distressed burnt umber line breaks up a large expanse of surface.

RIGHT

CAVE ART
PAINTING

The tones and textures of rustic pottery and ceramics complement a cave-art background above a limestone fire surround.

and enviable wall, floor or furniture finish for almost nothing. Gloss paint is intractable and there is nothing much you can do to it, except watch it drip, run and mark the floor indelibly.

NEW CLASSIC PAINTS

The new generations of traditionally inspired paints, however, are a very different matter. They vary, making generalization useless, but the reputable ones (such as American Stulb paints) give excellent coverage, and it is often possible to use just one coat; the new water-based paints are likely to be ecologically sound, causing none of the pungent problems peculiar to solvent-based types; they are adaptable and can be enhanced in a number of ways, with all the usual paint techniques as well as crackle glaze, sealer or polish.

If you want to be truly unique, you can make your own paint from start to finish. The main ingredients are simply colour or pigment mixed with a liquid base such as oil, varnish, or even water, together with a spot of gelatinous animal glue to bind it all together. It stops the pigment powdering away when the paint is dry. Milk tends not to be used as a base these days since its characteristic smell of rancid cheese offends most people. Most of the base colours are metal oxides dug from the ground – chrome yellow, red lead and zinc white for example. Raw umber from Umbria in Italy is heated to produce burnt umber and ultramarine is powdered lapis lazuli.

RIGHT
COLOUR AND
PATTERN

A dado is an obvious place to introduce pattern to a room, particularly where it is at eye level when you are seated. Here, English renaissance images juggle with balls in a simple mural design made by drawing round cardboard templates. The colours reflect the period; apricot and dusty rose being easily obtained by various mixings of raw and burnt sienna and yellow ochre. The rusting chair and earth-glazed pots underline the universality of iron oxides, as the tints in clay, as pigments, and as corrosion.

HOMEMADE PAINT

The central bowl of thick size paint is flanked by beeswax polish to the right and, from top to bottom; rabbit skin size granules, prepared hot size glue, PVA and dry mixed pigment. The recipe is: whiting 20 parts, viridian 1 part, neptune green 1 part, burnt umber ⅓ part.

HOT SIZE GLUE

1 cup rabbit-skin size

1 litre (1½ pints water)

Carbolic or boric acid

Leave the size in the water overnight to swell up. Then heat it in a bain-marie where it will liquefy ready for use. On cooling, this syrup will turn into a trembling jelly, so whenever you are working with it, keep a bain-marie nearby. Add a drop of carbolic acid or boric acid to stop it going rancid.

COLOURWASH PAINT

This generates a rich, coarse finish when size paint is used.

For each colour you will need:

1 part pigment

1 part hot size glue (see above)

5 parts water

Put the pigment in a bowl; add the glue and water, and mix. A pint of each mix should be enough for the average-sized room.

GLAZE RECIPE

1 part PVA adhesive

1 part paint

2 parts tap water

Mix together the PVA adhesive, paint and tap water and stir well. The adhesive will look white in the tin but when applied it becomes transparent. First, apply a base coat of white silk emulsion to the surface being decorated. Next, prepare a glaze with the darkest colour paint. Brush on with a 10 cm (4-inch) brush, concentrating on a square metre (square yard) at a time because the glaze dries quickly. Push the glaze around in different directions to achieve a patchy effect.

When dry, mix the next glaze with a lighter colour tone and again push the mixture around in patches as before.

The third and final coat is applied without any adhesive in the glaze, using a very pale paint. Brush this coat on very thinly with a wide brush. This will soften the final effect.

THICK SIZE PAINT

1 part pigment

1 part hot size glue (see left)

Unsurpassable for decorating small objects and fine furniture, thick size paint has the consistency of gesso with the advantage of colour. Apply 5 or 6 layers. The end result is very strong and can be polished or waxed.

Mix the pigment and size glue together and keep warm in a bain-marie while you work. If you want to eliminate the bain-marie and achieve a hard-wearing, waterproof finish for furniture, you can replace the glue with PVA adhesive mixed 50/50 with water.

DISTEMPER PAINT

A 5-litre (1 gallon) bucket

20 kilos (44 pounds) whiting

1/2 kilo (1 pound) tinting pigment (at least)

1.5 litres (2¼ pints) hot size glue (see above)

Distemper is the centuries-old traditional finish for interior walls and offers a chalky finish that emulsion fails to match, partly because distemper's pigment is just chalk. To colour distemper, add some pigment that has been mixed with water.

Sift the whiting into a bucket of water until a little cone of powder appears above the surface. Leave the brew overnight, then pour off the excess water. Stir in the hot glue and the paint is ready to use. This will make approximately 5 litres (1 gallon) of paint. To colour it, mix pigment with water until it forms a paste then add to paint.

AGEING WOOD

With the passing of time, paint gradually peels off and dust collects in the recesses of turned woodwork. To recreate this look, prime wood with a matt emulsion undercoat. Choose a pale colour for the initial application. When dry, brush on a liberal coating of beeswax polish straight from the tin. Over this, gently apply a second coat of paint in a darker shade. The moment it is touch-dry, sand it off.

The paint will peel off in places, revealing the first coat beneath. Dust sanding residue off with a dry brush.

Beeswax should then be mixed with Fuller's Earth (1.5 parts wax to one part powder), applied with a stiff brush and worked into cracks and recesses. After five minutes, the excess should be removed and polished with a duster.

ABOVE

COLOURWASH PAINT

Three bowls of colourwash paint (see opposite for recipe) sit on a surface showing the three successive layers that have been applied: yellow ochre, red ochre, burnt umber — each brushed out well to create a thin veil of colour.

LEFT

HOT SIZE GLUE

The glue (see opposite for recipe) is taken from the bain-marie and spooned on to the powder. The enamel dish itself will sit on the boiler to keep the paint warm and fluid.

DINING ROOMS &
EATING AREAS

TREEHOUSE

An airy invitation to spring and proof that small is beautiful — a tiny all-purpose room in a thicket of beech and oak. This is a place of dreams, the perfect escape from the banalities of everyday life, where delicate birdsong and dappled sunshine are perfectly complemented by a Bacchic diet of grapes and wine.

DINING ROOMS
& EATING AREAS

ating is, for most people, one of life's great pleasures, with the added bonus that everyone can do it, and can do it often – criteria which do not necessarily apply to other pleasurable pastimes. The fact that we eat every day, and several times a day, can make us blasé about the business. This is a pity, because in creative hands food preparation becomes an art only slightly less elevated than painting. Everything, from the precise quality and arrangement of the ingredients, to the choice of bowls and dishes, linen and glass, lighting, chairs, tablecloth and music, can work together to turn a humble meal into an unforgettable ceremony. The presentation of food, and the eating of it, are opportunities to make memories. The whole event has a pace of production much like a piece of theatre, and sharing a meal is the best excuse to sit down together as a group, enjoy each other's company, and indulge in that beleaguered old-fashioned activity, conversation.

Everyone can remember specific birthday teas, Thanksgiving dinners and Christmas lunches. Special meals become the markers of passing time and important events – an anniversary, as romantically candlelit as a seduction, the triumphant sound of popping corks to mark a work promotion or a celebratory wedding feast. From the Last Supper onwards, food has carried a weight of symbolism that insists on echoing quietly down the centuries.

On the other hand, unless you are Japanese, food is not a religious event. It is permissible to giggle, relax and have fun – you can even rock backwards in your chair and put your elbows on the table in some households. The place in which you eat exerts a strong influence on the mood of your meals. Some feel at ease with reams of dazzling napery and a glittering arsenal of cutlery. Most are happier with a motley collection of almost-matching plates and a homely checked tablecloth.

Good company is a vital ingredient for a successful meal, but there are material things that are conducive to a benign mood and good digestion. The most obvious is comfort — as anyone who has been seated on the collapsing chair with the edge of a table imprinting itself on his or her knees, will attest. When you sit down to eat, you do not want to do battle with the surroundings. You do not want cane chairs to ladder your tights, loose nails to rip your trousers, dogs to put inquisitive noses in improper places, or the light either to blind you or leave you troubled as to what you ate. Neither should the flower arrangement tickle your ears and isolate you behind a floral wall, or the voluminous tablecloth wind itself about your ankles and fell you as you try to stand up. You want enough space to be able to wield knife and fork, and the chair to be the right height. Not too much to ask.

If you eat in the kitchen, different standards apply from those which predominate if you are grand enough to have a separate dining room. For most people the dining room, like the traditional front parlour, is a room that, being little used, gathers a pervasive smell of damp and neglect. A dining room can be a troublesome thing. It implies that you have a retinue of staff who slave away behind the scenes to inflate your soufflé to the correct volume. Since this person in reality is likely to be your or your partner, it seems preferable, and more sociable, to eat where you cook. The disadvantage of this system is that when you drop the scalding casserole and have to ladle its contents back from the floor, you will have no secrets to hide from your guests.

PLANNING A DINING AREA

Having decided whether you will eat among the unwashed pans, or in splendid separation from the sordid, the next consideration is the style of your dining area. The classic country style revolves about a solid, sizeable pine table, which can don calendered damask for occasional grandeur, but is perfectly amenable to dents and spills, homework and the sewing machine. Four legs and no wobble are the essential criteria for a sense of security. An old pine table with cutlery drawers is attractive and useful, but try sitting at it before you decide to buy —

RIGHT

MEDITERRANEAN WARMTH

This has to be the countrified ideal of the good life. Sweet peas, scabious and cornflowers on the table, shelled fresh vegetables ready for lunch, while the sun streams in at the door. However, this idyll is to be found in London, and the shining expanse of polished wood furniture was collected during a lifetime of European travel, including a Welsh grandfather clock, a French fruitwood table, and a Spanish yoke over the door.

often the depth required to house the drawer means that your circulation is cut off at the thighs and that you cannot cross your legs.

It is a good idea to have a dining table as big and heavy as you can possibly accommodate. Solidity is a wonderful thing in a dining table. A rickety table is as maddening as a squeaking bed, and ingenious arrangements with extra leaves often suffer from instability.

The worst of all possible dining room scenarios conjures up young memories of a polished rosewood Regency table with flaps, shrouded on all normal occasions apparently with felt underlay and a plastic mackintosh. Possibly its naked glory was revealed to a few discerning and highly civilized adults, but I never saw it without its overcoat. Country furniture should be robust enough to cope with real life and to bear its scars with dignity. At its best, the kitchen/dining table is the focus of the creative energy of the whole house – this is where letters are written and Christmas dough decorations are made.

FLOORING AND SEATING FOR EATING AREAS

It makes sense, then, to ensure that the floor is easy to clean. This, for most families, obviates rugs, carpet or matting. Smoothly finished floorboards, sealed cork, tiles, slate, stone and good old-fashioned linoleum are congenial underfoot, and do not object to an occasional mulch of juice and crushed peas. Dining room seating needs serious consideration. If you enjoy lengthy and protracted meals, lingering over coffee as an excuse to keep on talking, then it is essential to practice sprawling in the prospective chairs. You may discover that your legs get up to all sorts of twisting and crossing and that you are lost without struts at ankle level. Classic Windsor chairs fulfil most criteria of comfort and simple elegance, whereas some modern dining chairs have aggressive vertical backs in the style of Charles Rennie Mackintosh that transport you to the days of whalebone stays, or protruding knobs where the legs attach, or hard square seats designed to dent your thighs. Heavy and unwieldy seats are a nuisance to shift, and wicker, which is comfortable, creaky and user-friendly, usually takes up too much room and has a penchant for tearing your tights. Antique benches have an

institutional air, no matter how elegant they are. But the unusual Scandinavian bench seats that expand to become box-beds are roomy, comfortable and practical.

LIGHTING UP

Good lighting is the next essential. A central ceiling light is not as desirable as it might seem. Rise-and-fall pendant lights which are a common solution, have a propensity to either shine in your eyes or block your view. To avoid this, you could try one of the Victorian handkerchief shades with a skirt that softens the glare. This will focus the light in a narrower beam, directly below the lampshade. Another solution that looks pretty when unlit, but does not really shed a flattering light, is the Paul Revere punched tin shade, or the Shaker wrought iron candelabra fitted with real candles or electric fakes. This would also be the best place for your glittering cut-glass chandelier, especially if it is resplendent with coloured glass drops in the shape of fruit. They are all lovely objects, their one fault is that they are not efficient sources of light. For the best of both worlds, enjoy your fancy light fixtures for their charm and character, and use additional lighting for your main sources. Ceramic uplighters on the wall give a soft, all-round reflected illumination that is both useful and kind.

SOFT CANDLELIGHT

Candles on the table cast the dependable warm glow for which they have become a cliché – again you have to be vigilant about their height. Your family heirloom Regency candlesticks look magnificent, but they will effectively obliterate the person opposite. If you do want conversation to flow across as well as along, you will do better to use a crowd of short, stubby candles, nightlights in coloured or cut-glass lanterns, or floating candles, their light twinkling from among flower heads for a serious touch of over-the-top romance. If you are going to use candles, be generous with them – beeswax or a high stearin content guarantee slow-burning and good behaviour. Decent, cheap candles are available in large quantities from many household stores.

OPPOSITE ABOVE LEFT

GREEN BEAMS

This all-purpose room in a Somerset dairy has dark wooden beams on the ceiling and green-painted ones on the walls, in keeping with the local tradition.

OPPOSITE ABOVE RIGHT

DARKLY ROMANTIC

Original William Morris wallpaper is darkened still further with a tinted colourwash, as well as weighty brocade curtains falling in heavy folds from a mahogany curtain pole.

OPPOSITE BELOW LEFT

COSY VICTORIANA

Scones, clotted cream and home-made jam complemented by a kettle on the hob and blazing logs on the fire – this is one of life's great fattening pleasures.

OPPOSITE BELOW RIGHT

BARONIAL SPLENDOUR

A medieval building is given all the drama it deserves with a dark polished slate floor, a painted gallery and an inferno of flames from the massive stove reflected in a wrought iron candelabra.

HEDGEROW
COLLECTION

*A sideboard overflows with
spring flowers — poppies and
elderflowers, roses and
cranesbill.*

During a power cut, it may have occurred to you that it would be a
good idea to use those attractive brass and glass paraffin lamps that you
have collected. Having endured their noxious fumes and cleaned the
blackened ceiling, you will wonder that our predecessors survived at
all with such lamps as their only source of light, and put them thankfully
back in the attic. They are in fact much more suitable for outdoor use.
Put them on a table for al fresco suppers in the garden, where the smell
can dissipate and leave you air to breathe.

MOOD LIGHTING

To add glamorous glitter to your windows at Christmas, or to create a cheerful twinkle in a dark corner at any time, you can deck a twiggy leafless branch or a dried giant hogweed with white fairy lights – not serious illumination, but an uplift to the spirits. Along the same lines, big low-wattage clear globe-shaped bulbs strung at different points from visible looped flex attached to the ceiling give a punctuated brightness and a sparkly and incandescent air of gaiety.

The room in which you eat probably needs the widest range of alternative lighting – memorable meals depend very much on mood, and mood-setting is what lighting is all about. If you have an all-purpose table on which you practice lino-cutting as well as haute cuisine, you will want to be able to call on a bright, clear light as well as a flattering dim glow. If you eat in the kitchen, you need bright light in the area where you prepare food, but it is also useful to be able to make the unwashed pans disappear temporarily by turning off the light there, leaving the table in its own pool of light.

FUNCTIONAL FURNITURE

In a cottage, this all-important room will have to serve many functions – the walls may be lined with dressers or sideboards, and old sagging armchairs may do patient duty, their floral cretonne covers faded and worn by the years. This is a thoroughly respectable country look, not to be sniffed at. If you can run to an eighteenth-century Windsor settee with homespun cushions to soften its seat and a dresser painted Scandinavian falun red, you will have achieved the country ideal.

COLOURFUL DINING

As so often, an inspired use of colour is what distinguishes the room where Sunday lunch merges imperceptibly with supper, from the one where a hasty exodus takes place as soon as the plates are cleared. Most dining rooms have a preponderance of brown. There tends to be more wood per square centimetre (inch) in a dining room than anywhere else in the house, and this is something to look at critically. Brown is peaceful and soothing and will not upset the digestion but it is at its most beautiful in contrast with colour – from warm off-white at the most inoffensive end of the spectrum, to mutable colour-washed russet at the most vibrant.

Warm reds work well in a dining room, as do all the colours beloved of the Swedes and Shakers. Tongued-and-grooved walls appreciate a touch of colour, and the dining room is a classic setting for panelled walls – easily achieved with a mitre and wooden moulding.

ALMOST ORIENTAL

This room which belongs to a furniture designer and maker combines peasant solidity with oriental sophistication and simplicity. The quality of the materials is accentuated against a puritan background of white tiles to make the wood look more weathered and grainy, the slate more sumptuous and polished. Even the cheese looks more cheesy, while the lettuce is positively frivolous.

WALL STENCILS

Up until the invention of affordable wallaper in the nineteenth century, stencils were the only means of embellishing bare walls, enabling elegant patterns to be repeated over and over again in stripes and borders or as decorative punctuation. They had, and still have, a great advantage over wallpaper in that stencilled patterns can be customized to fit and accentuate the particular quirks and character of a room.

Windows, picture rails and fireplaces can all be flattered with a border. Colours can complement or contrast with one another, and motifs can be altered to suit different applications – a stencil can be enlarged and the shapes made bolder to accommodate a change of scale, from lacquer box to ceiling swag, for example.

Stencils have a liveliness of finish that no machine-made paper can match. The ease with which you can create cloudy subtleties of mutable colour ensure their status as a classic decorative technique.

When stencilling techniques were rediscovered in the late 1970s, they were excitedly seized upon by the decorating world. However, they subsequently suffered several pitfalls which have given them something of an enduring bad name. The main disaster areas concerned an over proliferation of flowers and a timidity with and insensitive use of, colour and texture. Many stencilled floral and figurative motifs tend to look dated, because in order to stylize them into useable and recognizable stencils, they edge towards an uncomfortable and unconvincing Art Nouveau look. Generally speaking, geometric or architectural details are better and more stylish on walls, while stencilled flowers are most at home on small objects, where they can be combined with découpage to their mutual enrichment.

Stencils lend themselves well to bold repetitions, grand rope swags and witty *trompe-lòeil* brackets and finials. But they must be big enough to hold their own.

DRESSER DISPLAY
*A speckled Italian
spongeware bowl is
complemented by Joanna
Still plates on either side;
while the white spotted bowls
come from Annecy in France.
A paisley stencil complements
a motif on a favourite
tablecloth.*

MEDIEVAL WALL

This abbey-inspired wall decoration gets its punch from the use of a dark background to bolster and contain the vine, and the stylized detail of the strawberries and leaves.

DECORATIVE WALLS

Many people like the idea of stencils but do not really have the courage of their convictions. A timid frieze of pallid pansies clinging to the ceiling coving will make no-one's heart skip a beat. Whereas a delicious paisley design in warm purple and spice colours on an ochre background, mellowed with an ageing glaze, will give you a lift.

This wall (left and below) was inspired by paintings on a medieval wall in Mulcheney Abbey in Somerset. A vine and strawberry motif climbs up within the confines of broad stripes, with a Gothic abstract ermine design (the spidery images) punctuating the spaces between.

1 The design can be stencilled directly on to distempered or emulsioned walls. On distemper walls always work in distemper, size paint or in artists' gouache. Paint background stripes in solid colour, then pencil in the outlines faintly, using a spirit level. Then apply stencil. Keep it in place with masking tape and use a stiff brush to stipple through water-based paint.

2 Freehand, join the leaves to the vine and embellish them. Use a ruler, pencil and spirit level to mark out the ermine design; paint it freehand and, when dry, sand lightly to disguise any rough workmanship or harsh outlines that remain.

3 Use off-white paint to 'spot' the strawberries and edge the leaves swiftly with short strokes from a sable brush to imitate the serrated edge of the strawberry leaf.

4 The finished work is indistinguishable from hand-painted decoration but is completed in a fraction of the time. Rub lightly with sandpaper or wash a thin colour over the top for an authentic dusty look.

CHAPTER FOUR

KITCHENS & PANTRIES

KITCHENS & PANTRIES

Kitchens are the heart of the house. They have to work harder than any other room, and they are also subject to the most changes of use – the transition from Butler sink to a state-of-the-art dishwasher has to be accommodated; the replacement fridge-freezer, double the size of its predecessor, has to be made room for; even the acquisition of a large casserole may cause storage problems. There is more essential clutter in a kitchen than in any other room, and generally there is more clutter than you ever thought you would need to find a home for. So the vital consideration, before you give a thought to stencilled swags of grapes, is storage.

Kitchens of antiquity and modest rural peasant examples, consist of a source of water – which may be a bucket; a source of heat – which could have a distinct similarity to a barbecue; and whatever pots, pans and crockery exist, proudly displayed. In Africa, wooden spoons and light bulbs are laid out as objects of beauty. In South America, enamel bowls and plates, resplendent with exotic stencilled flora are ranged on the walls. Looking at them, one has an uneasy sense that less may indeed be more, and that to have too much is to court a restless feeling of dissatisfaction. The trouble is, that though one may only use the fish-kettle once a year, there is no substitute when you do want to use it, and that for the rest of the year it has to go somewhere. Ditto the asparagus pan, the bun tins, the semi-successful salad dryer and the serrated knives that have lost their edge. And then there is all the ugly twentieth-century paraphernalia of yellowing plastic electrical objects – the ice-cream maker, the food processor, the fruit juicer, the beige toaster with timid wheatsheaf design, and most common in a series of contemporary visual abominations – the plastic electric kettle, designed to be just too tall to fit under the tap, and to age rapidly and hideously.

It is strongly tempting to throw the whole lot out, and return to the

SINGEING THE BLUES

A triumph of authentic original detail, this gloriously ornate polished brass and cast iron kitchen range has always been part of this woodman's cottage. Here, generations of work-clothes have been hung on the rail beneath the mantelpiece to become imbued with smoky warmth. The perfect partnership of Spode and denim is a twentieth-century inspiration and a great example of the innocent fun of decorating.

pestle and mortar, the mandoline, the potato ricer – all of which have collectible appeal. But that would be foolhardy and expensive. The answer lies in editing.

ORGANIZING KITCHEN EQUIPMENT

The most important kitchen items that are in constant use must undergo a charm test – if they look good and fit in with the prevailing colour scheme, they can stay visible. If not, hide them. This goes for anything plastic – and the worst aspect of plastic things is that they always have trailing bits and extra attachments. These fall out of cupboards and require further hideousness in the form of specially designed plastic holders to keep them under control. If they are essential to your life, a resigned sigh and an ingenious use of cupboard space is your best recourse. If not, joining forces with a friend and bestowing your excess bounty on a garage sale is fun, and a satisfying way to lose unwanted impedimenta. It is a good idea to take a hard critical look at your kitchen equipment occasionally, and ruthlessly throw out anything you do not use. After a respectable period you could probably pass on the melamine trays which were given to you as wedding presents. Occasional-use objects could be relegated to the attic, cellar or cupboard under the stairs, particularly if you are an orderly sort of person who will remember where you put them.

DISPLAYING COLLECTIONS

Next you should deal with the beautiful things that you treasure – the Portuguese bowls and Welshware jugs for example. These should be the clue to your entire decorative scheme. Blue and white may preponderate – a good kitcheny partnership that works with wood-browns, reds and sunny yellows. You may have a collection of rich green fruit plates, or Staffordshire jugs, or floral teapots. As always, the wise thing to do is flaunt it, if it gives you pleasure. Not everything all at once, but colour-related pieces which you can echo and play up in your walls and painted furniture.

There is a fine line to be drawn between eclectic richness and

EVOLUTIONARY
KITCHEN
The very serious professional French chef's cooker and designer radiator indicate that this kitchen was not put together on a small budget. However, it flaunts a casual, spontaneous air with its beautifully fitted disparate drawers and artfully aged paint on walls and woodwork. It should not succeed but it does, mainly because of the unifying framework of untreated wood and clever details such as the uniformly spaced matching drawer handles and the general similarity of colour and texture – not identical, but related.

THE QUINTESSENTIAL COUNTRY KITCHEN

This country kitchen is practical and unpretentious, displaying a dash of nostalgic charm with its faux Victorian style. Reproduction tiles, brass taps and a butler sink with a weathered wooden draining board are used to create the look. The pans are clean and bright without being dauntingly new and there is an attractive mixture of the rustic and oriental.

claustrophobic excess. Stalactites of dusty herbs hanging from the beams, shelves jostling with a plethora of slightly sticky and chipped china bric-a-brac, corn dollies, greasy with years of kitchen duty, faded dried flower arrangements and rosemary wreaths blurred with spiders' webs all add up to an asthmatic's nightmare and need a fierce purge. It is surprising how easily one becomes inured to one's surroundings, and no longer sees the objects which make up the environment. The secret of pleasurable appreciation is that it is better to have just one sprightly slipware dish proudly displayed on a colourwashed russet dresser, than an ill-assorted multitude. Always play up objects on display with the decor of the dresser or shelves.

A cottage kitchen worthy of its name has to have a dresser. It is an essential part of the country ethos, and a necessary showcase for the

best of your ceramics, riding trophies, invitations and strangely undulating clay ashtrays made by your nephew. Glass-fronted cupboards have the same country charm, particularly if they are given an interesting paint-finish and the shelves are edged with pretty paper or leather, or filet lace. They have an advantage against the classic open-shelved dresser in that their contents are protected from the inevitable kitchen grime. In a perfect world, every kitchen would smell of lavender and sparkle with polish – most people are too busy these days to give this room more than a cursory once-over with a damp cloth whenever the place begins to look unduly dog-eared.

It makes sense to protect as much as possible behind cupboard doors or glass. The otherwise charming narrow shelf around the wall just below the ceiling – a favourite Arts and Crafts device – is particularly

CULINARY COMFORT

This is a sophisticated pastiche of a farmhouse kitchen: by no means huge, the addition of a fat kilim-covered armchair instantly gives it a sense of space and leisure; the rise-and-fall airer festooned with tea-cloths and the handsome milk and butter containers are countrified touches. But Mophead apple-decked trees and naive art suggest a city mentality. The combination is fresh and welcoming.

CLASSIC INGREDIENTS

Everyone loves blue and white, and this, the country kitchen of a food writer, is a perfect example of how it should be done: hand-painted Mexican tiles make an airy frame for a handsome cobalt-blue cooker, the plethora of transfer-printed china is complemented by simple custom-built shelves of warm pine and a splash of Schiaparelli pink roses brings the whole room alive. The lighting — always an Achilles heel in otherwise splendid interiors — is inventive and original. Whether or not it works, since it has to be powered by a generator in this remote spot, is another matter, but there is an air of romance about the place and candles are on hand should starlight prove inadequate.

SCARLET AGA

If you have it, flaunt it. A sizzling reaction to a shiny red Aga is to electrify it in partnership with a stinging complementary green. Cheap Chinese enamelware with bold stencilled flowers echoes the colour combination, as do sea kale and radishes, for a relentlessly colour-cued decorative scheme.

PAINTED CUPBOARDS

Freehand prancing birds of indeterminate species and overflowing urns decorate the cupboard doors in this painter's kitchen. The meandering red frieze, the tiles and the shutters are all in keeping with a green and red theme, which has a natural affinity with fruit and vegetables. The ceramic Belfast sink has an antiquated mixer tap. An elegant and excellent design which is often found, in sparkling chrome, in kitchens and hospitals, where single-handed efficiency in difficult situations is essential.

vulnerable to collecting grease and grime wafted up on kitchen thermals. Keep washable things up there on display, and remember to wash them frequently. At all costs do not put your books on high shelves, because they will become unpleasantly sticky in no time at all.

KITCHEN STORAGE

Kitchens need every variety of cupboard, shelf and drawer for which you have room. Any fitted kitchen catalogue will show you a good range of ingenious ideas for tables that fold out from the walls, ironing boards that disappear into the moulding, narrow cupboards that trundle out bearing a ton of tins, rubbish receptacles that look like drawer fronts, dishwashers and fridges that look like cupboards and a multitude of things that look like other things and behave in surprising ways.

There is a lively debate about the relative merits of the fitted versus the higgledy-piggledy eclectic kitchen: fitted kitchens tend to lack character, but a junkyard of mismatched furniture lacks almost everything else. As usual, in compromise lies sanity — as large an area of unbroken worktop as possible makes for serene cooking. Solid, stable dressers are practical and worth their weight in gold. Wall-hung cupboards are useful and enable you to hide more kitchen clutter, but the essence of a good country look is that it must age well — most chipboard carcasses with wood fronts look dire after a year or two. On the other hand, they are cheeringly easy to paint over (after an initial sanding to provide a key: Shaker paint works very well and bear dents and scratches uncomplainingly) and if you replace their horrible fiddly brass ring handles with ceramic or brass knobs, they will all cohere in an inoffensive way. Panels of punched tin in the classic American style can be used to jazz up cupboard fronts, while unpretentious doors of painted tongued-and-grooved pine have a countrified farmhouse air.

Good doors and handsome surfaces make a huge difference, but no matter how much energy you expend on embellishing, painting, liming or rag-rolling their fronts, ready-made fitted kitchen elements will never look like objects of beauty in themselves. At the other extreme, there are those people who would rather adapt antique cupboards to hold plumbing and a Belfast sink in order to have a view of uninterrupted antiquity. This kind of faking has to be done well to look good and to be practical.

SINKS AND BASINS

Water has a way of trickling into nooks and crannies, and may ruin the surface of old wood. And the bitter truth is that Belfast sinks are beasts except for filling watering cans and washing Wellington boots. For anything more delicate, they just cause trouble. On the whole, this kind of attempt to avoid the commonplace works better as a plinth for a basin in a bathroom, than for the hard-working kitchen sink. Hardwood draining boards, twice as large as you think you need, make an effective and good-looking sink surround.

Stainless steel sinks with integral draining boards are not beautiful, but they are forgivable and do not pretend to be other than they are, and you can give them a good scrub without fear of damaging something precious. Ceramic sinks, as I have said previously, are handsome but infuriating – they are difficult to clean because they usually have insufficiently rounded corners to be reachable, they chip easily, and they break your favourite spongeware at the slip of a finger. And as they are normally set, there is a blatantly germ-infested edged of soggy wood between them and the draining board. Coloured enamel sinks lose their shine unless you treat them like Spode figurines. Sinks of white corian are discreet and well-behaved, but they generally seem to have problems in the plug department. You cannot beat an ordinary plug, which keeps water in the sink when it is in place, and lets it out when you remove it. Modern sinks come with a more rarefied kind of plug that does everything except hold water. This can be intensely irritating if you are trying to scrub mussels or wash lettuces.

KITCHEN FLOORING

Since the kitchen is the domain of dough bits and spilled tea, it is essential that the floor can be swept easily and washed when need be. Textured flooring is a magnet to encrusted crumbs and dirt – the

TRIBAL TOUCHES
A modern kitchen attached to a nineteenth-century cottage has had its newness muted by the use of worn flagstones rescued from a vicarage, an old-fashioned cream-coloured Aga cooker and wood-framed windows. The window-seat is a wonderful invention, serving as a comfortable perch from which to view the world, and a secret storage area. Cream walls and grey-blue woodwork are a soothing colour combination which might even verge on dullness were it not for the lightning-patterned Afghan kilim on the floor and ethnic treasures on every surface.

SHELF DISCIPLINE

Collections are no fun unless you can gloat over them, and this pantry filled with jugs and candlesticks is the perfect anteroom. The jugs are not on public display all the time, but they are accessible and visible when you want them to be. High narrow shelves like this are a space-saving way of displaying treasures, but are best avoided in kitchens, where rising air bears a lot of unwanted grease.

kitchen floor has to be smooth. All the classic finishes work well — terracotta pamments, polished slate, cork and worn stone. Some bright Mexican tiles are hardy enough for use on the floor and can cheer a winter day. Painted floors are fun in a kitchen, where you stain or paint floorboards in plain colours, stripes or faux tiles. You can spatter the floor with a jazzy pattern of colour if you are feeling bold, or paint or stencil borders and repeating patterns. If the permanence of floor paints is too daunting, you could simply paint a floorcloth — known as colonial linoleum by passionate restorers because of its eighteenth-century American connections — and indulge in a painterly frenzy that can be whipped out of sight when it gets too much. Polished concrete has its fans, though this is a matter for advanced experiment. Linoleum, invigorated with an occasional paraffin wash, is a warm and tough floor

HEAVILY PLATED

If you happen to own a vast collection of plates, then you need a rack such as this. There is nothing particularly exceptional in this room, but all the elements work together harmoniously — the handsome panelled cupboard, the polished floor and the plate rack are made of similar butterscotch-coloured wood, which contrasts well with the aquamarine of door and seascape. Baskets always look good in a kitchen.

finish. It can be found in handsome strong plain colours, and interesting, slightly dappled designs. Vinyl is not so good — usually it seems to have a surface which is both sticky and greasy, a distinct disadvantage in a kitchen. Small washable rugs, rag rugs or runners in the Swedish style soften acres of shiny flooring, and can be placed to define cosy sitting areas, as opposed to busy food preparation areas.

COOKERS AND GRILLS

There is little one can do to disguise the uncountrified ugliness of some kitchen essentials. Shiny new cookers work well, and one would not wish a moody and demanding iron range on any but the most dedicated of rural authentics. Industrial cookers are handsome and basic, with a masculine integrity that fits in well with the general honesty of country interiors, but they are costly. If you can accustom yourself to a wholly different way of cooking, solid fuel cookers, and their modern gas and electric equivalents have the right rugged good looks, and provide the irresistible warm heart to the house. They can also be induced to heat water and radiators.

Old-fashioned enamel gas cookers from the 1940s are sometimes preferable to their modern equivalents and will have stood the test of time. Modern cookers tend to look tatty surprisingly quickly – metal trim strips get dog-eared, knobs fall off and transfer numerals on the dials are worn away by minimal cleaning. Microchip technology has not advanced cooker design significantly in the last 50 years, and the materials used in new cookers are not as robust as they used to be.

WORKTOPS, LIGHTING AND ATMOSPHERE

The most congenial worktops are made of wood, tiles, slate, or marble if money is no object. The fewer bits and pieces you need in the way of pastry boards, chopping boards and mats for hot casseroles, the simpler and more efficient life will be. Of course it all has to be easy to clean, and the usual worktop clutter can be alleviated by the simple device of a raised narrow shelf on which to put all the spices and oil bottles that can otherwise encroach on precious workspace.

Kitchen lighting needs to be as adaptable as possible. Strip lighting over worktops is hard to better as a practical source of light by which to work, but it is horrible to behold. A lip under overhanging cupboards will shield its glare, or you could investigate strips of punched tin which are prettier. Pendant lights over a worktop look attractive, but they can get in the way, and the shades must be washable. Recessed spotlights are acceptable in kitchens and shed light where you want it.

A comfortable kitchen is a relaxed place in which to cook, eat and converse with friends and family. Lighting, seating and music should all contribute to this end. Flowers on the table, favourite china on the walls, simple checked curtains keeping out the sight of winter rain and a braided rag rug on the floor – these are all guarantees that you will never have to cook alone.

TRAYS ELEGANT

A collection of favourite trays and colanders belonging to a potter hang on a wall in his home, which is an ancient restored forge.

TRADITIONAL
OILED FLOORCLOTHS

Floorcloths – painted and sealed canvas mats – developed from the oilcloth jackets and capes used by the traditional barnacled seafarers to keep salt water out and warmth in. Thickly varnished and impervious to water and dirt, floorcloths became the perfect solution for practical and decorative flooring from the mid-seventeenth century onwards They were made from canvas which was painted with layers of linseed oil and rosin and coloured with such pigments such as white-lead and lamp black, umber and verdigris. They were cheap and easy to make, transportable and could be as decorative as the artistry of their maker allowed. Floorcloths did not last forever, and had a tendency to crack, but these were minor faults compared with the disadvantage of cold and draughty bare floorboards. In time, linoleum became the commercially manufactured flooring answer and homemade floorcloths fell by the wayside.

But something of their spirit still appeals. Floor tends to resist decor – you can paint them and stencil them, and in fact just about anything that works on walls can be made to work on floors. But somehow, while tackling the walls of an entire room seems an manageable prospect, painting the floor does not. For a start, you have to empty the room completely. Then you have to have good floorboards or smooth concrete. The idea of waiting for layer after layer of protective varnish to dry will seem more and more unthinkable, and the though of the irrevocable marks and mistakes in your design that you will never be able to remove will become more and more daunting. Finally you will give up the whole lunatic notion and think 'well, why not just sand the floorboards to show off their battered charm?'

Floorcloths, on the other hand, do not have to be painted in situ. You can hardly drag the kitchen floor out to the garage, but a roll of canvas is perfectly portable. You can make it as small or as enormous as you

FANCY FLOORING

Many of Natalie Woolf's floorcloth designs use variations on a favourite theme she has developed. She uses a stencil for the basic shapes and then experiments with different colours and different layers of colour, with wildly different results. Herein lies the joy of floorcloth painting – the basic materials are not expensive and playing with contrasts and tones is a pleasure in itself.

like since canvas comes in generous widths, which can be joined together if you are contemplating fitting a ballroom. Strange sizes and shapes are no problem, though curves are tricky to finish neatly. And the most enjoyable part is the painting – you can do anything you like, using any combination of colours; you can paint freehand, print, spatter or stencil; you can distress the crisp finished motifs, you can enrich the finish with colourwashes; you can create a tightly geometric pattern like the fake tiles of the seventeenth century, or indulge in a swirling pattern a la Matisse; you can fake a family crest; plagiarize a Versailles tapestry, invent a trompe-l'oeil tassels and fringes, copy elegant lettering to commemorate auspicious personal events or paint a portrait of your favourite pet. The whole world is at your feet

RIGHT

The finished floorcloth is predominantly blue and orange with touches of bright yellow, burgundy, green and indigo. The design is simple yet sophisticated, with clean graceful curves, crisply regimented by indigo stripes.

Soft, quaint, old-fashioned colours make an asymmetrical floorcloth of muted intensity. It takes courage to put together unlikely combinations such as this blue and orange, but it works beautifully. With cheap materials such as canvas, the risks of experimenting are minimal, and the rewards magnificent.

Stronger, richer colours in an asymmetrical layout are brought to life by a maverick patch of sunny yellow.

INSTRUCTIONS

You will need:

Double duck, sailcloth or canvas

Vinyl primer

PVA adhesive,

double sided tape or a sewing machine and

strong thread to finish the edges.

Fabric glue

Vinyl matt emulsion in your chosen colours.

Small details can be painted in

acrylic artists paint.

Brushes, sponges, masking tape for straight lines,

pencils, carbon paper,

stencils, templates etc.

Clear or tinted satin-finish water-based varnish,

of which you will need at least three coats.

Set square and long ruler — you can use a

newspaper to perfect a right angle.

Scalpel

Begin by painting the canvas with a coat of primer. Allow it to dry, and then paint on two patchy layers of base coat, using indigo and black matt emulsion mixed together. Take the paint over the edges of the floorcloth. Let each individual coat dry before continuing. Draw the outline of the design to fit your cloth, using a set square to mark right-angled corners, and the ruler to ensure straight edges. Allow 2.5 cm (1 in) all round for the hem. Cut the four corners to make a mitre. To obtain a crisp edge, score the fabric very lightly along the fold line with a ruler and scalpel. Apply fabric glue and

fold. Pinch along the fold line and hold the canvas in place with weights or bulldog clips.

When the glue is dry, apply the tulip design (see opposite) using carbon paper templates, and cover the eventual indigo stripes with masking tape. Paint background colours for the broad stripes freehand, using one or two shades and avoiding the tulips. Take the colour over the edge of the cloth again. Paint the tulips with a fine brush to suit the rest of the design. Sand back to reveal the cloudy layers of colour beneath. Allow to dry. Next apply at least three generous layers of varnish, allowing them to dry completely between layers.

Use a grant projector, a magnifying photocopier or a grid to enlarge the tulip design, or do it freehand. If you enclose it within a square, it will be easier to position equidistantly on the floorcloth. Place the tulips by eye, or measure and calculate heir position for a more regular design.

Once you are happy with the design, you can paint out anything that severely displeases you, or mitigate colour that is too strong with diluted paint or by sanding it back to the base coat. And the most exciting moment comes once you have finished your design, and you give the whole thing – which looks somewhat dull and flat – a coat of varnish. Suddenly the colours spring to life and assume a richness, depth and sparkle that will inspire you with plans for hall runners, kitchen mats and bathroom rugs.

FAR LEFT

Work in progress - prime the floorcloth, and give it two coats of indigo mixed with black. Position the masking tape and transfer the design onto the cloth.

LEFT

Paint the tulips and give the cloth a coat of secondary colours. Use a combination of sponged colour and sanding back to achieve an interesting broken effect. Finish with three coats of satin-finish water-based varnish.

CHAPTER FIVE

BEDROOMS &
GUEST ROOMS

BEDROOMS & GUEST ROOMS

Country bedrooms are a refuge from the world. They should be private and sacrosanct, the place where you can indulge your decorative dreams. If a monastic cell is the tranquil haven to which you aspire, then that is what you can create. If ruched chintz is your secret desire, then no-one can stop you from festooning walls and windows with billowing roses.

You can take risks with colour in pursuit of your fantasy. After all, most people do not spend a huge amount of time in their bedrooms. You have no-one to please but yourself, and whoever shares the room with you. Colour-coordination should not imply having everything in the same colours, which tends to look obsessive and gives an air of a museum collection. It works best when a few colours dominate, and are echoed in subtly differing tones of paint and fabric. Choosing a style of dècor for the bedroom can be a source of bitter contention. The consensus seems to be that a bedroom is the woman's domain. It is unlikely that the country standard of lace-bedecked bed would be any red-blooded man's dearest wish, yet some shared bedrooms are indeed all frills and furbelows.

Textiles come into their own in rustic bedrooms: soft surfaces, warm covers, bedding, curtains, rugs and carpets all add up to comfort, which is of primary importance. This is the place in which you can exploit the magic capacity of different textiles to merge in mutual flattery. Antique paisley is always glorious, but it becomes sublime when partnered with Turkish rugs and floral prints in toning colours. You can embellish such a scheme with foxy red walls, heavy damask curtains, blinds of old ivory linen edged with tea-darkened lace, cushions of tapestry mellowed by time and dark tartan bedlinen in sympathetic colours. A good sprinkling of tassels and braid will lend further weight and glamour. Or you might sleep sweeter in

SHEER SIMPLICITY

A slice of sunlight emphasizes an extravagance of utterly romantic bedding – frilled organdy pillow-cases; embriodered linen pillow slips; tape lace and appliqué cushions, and an antique quilt adorned with peonies and auriculas. Seductive ingredients for a Sleeping Beauty saga, particularly if the heroine is not averse to ironing.

surroundings of seaside blue and white; a look of simplicity and innocence reminiscent of youthful holidays by the sea. Try fresh, striped unlined curtains, bare polished floorboards and bedlinen in crisp blue and white checked cotton against a matt black or white-painted Victorian iron bed. The bedding can be covered for additional warmth in winter with a quilt made from indigo and white African resist-printed Adire cloth. Complete the scene with white walls, a rag rug showing a bobbing boat on a bouncing sea, a few favourite shells on the window-sill and a bunch of cornflowers in a white jug. You can consign any other precious textiles, such as embroidered runners or tablecloths, to do charming duty in a guest room.

BEDROOM QUILTS

Quilts are synonymous with a country bedroom. There are many countries around the world which have splendid quilt traditions, and there is nothing like a quilt to give instant character and warmth to a bedroom. But use them sparingly. A stack of quilts looks wonderful in a linen press, but in a bedroom it is a mistake to have one on the bed, one on the window-seat, another on the wall and a third draped fetchingly on the Pennsylvania Dutch blanket chest. Use one, or at most two, if they complement one another well. And remember that many of the best classic designs such as Log Cabin, most of the bold Amish designs, Irish Chain, Simple Blocks and Durham Strippy are very easy to make, and can be run up on a sewing machine. Even the quilting itself can be done by machine.

To achieve an authentic result, it is essential to use pure cotton or wool. The Shakers made whole cloth quilts with homespun checked wool, and they did not always quilt them; often they used the time-saving device of knotting together the pieces with bright thread. For the wadding, also use cotton or wool. Old blankets make a perfectly acceptable filling too. They hang well and do not need to be minutely quilted to stay in place. Faded fabrics find a good home in pieced quilt covers, but make sure that they are not just about to disintegrate completely. Unpretentious fabrics such as shirting stripes, subdued

RIGHT
INDIGO AND IVORY
A dawn chorus of oystercatchers and waders greets the occupant of this bedroom which looks out onto a peaceful estuary in Somerset, England. The indigo patchwork was dyed and stitched by the owner to resemble the handsome textiles woven by the Ewe people in Africa.

OVERLEAF
LOFTY IDEAL
The sunfilled attic bedroom in a modern purpose-built barn offers plenty of light and air and costs a fraction of a conventional building. A canvas chair, a couple of model yachts and the whimsical arabesques of an iron bed induce a feeling of seaside lightheartedness.

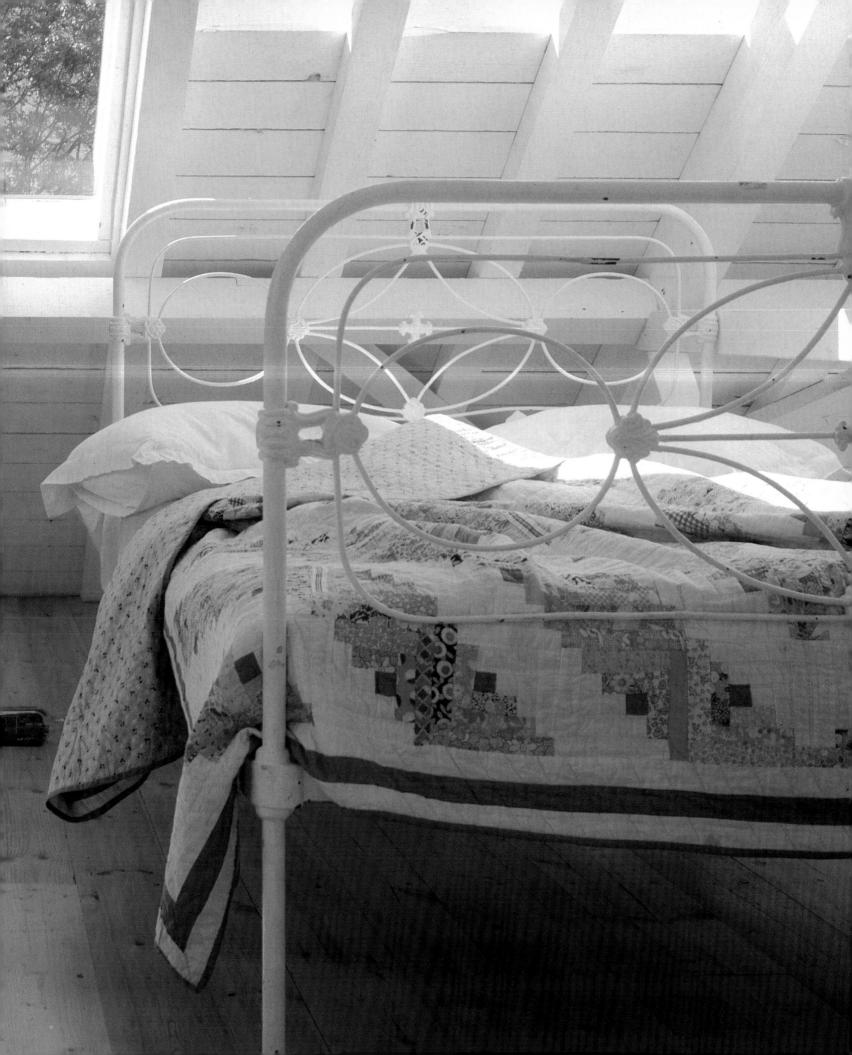

florals, checks, paisley and no-nonsense calico all work well in a country context.

There are some people who like to feel embraced and enclosed in a bedroom, and others who need light and air. Swedish box-beds enclosed with curtains are heaven for the former, a hammock beneath the stars is the answer for the latter. Often a couple consists of one of each persuasion, and cautious negotiation is the only way to resolve differing needs. Also, the changing seasons may demand different solutions. Filmy translucent curtains may seem like the perfect response to an energetic and early dawn chorus, but heavy quilted window hangings are utter luxury when the windows are etched with frost.

BEDROOM LAYOUT

Bedrooms tend to be under-used. With a little imagination, you can counter this and turn yours into a haven in which to read, write letters, and indulge in whimsical ruminations while stitching your tapestry. All hell may be crashing around downstairs, which gives all the more charm to your secret eyrie. An essential prerequisite for absolute perfection is an open fire. It need not be real, since gas fakes with pretend coal are convincing and shed lively warmth with no fuss. Somehow there is less comfort to be had from huddling round a radiator, than curling up in front of a fire. Gas fires are just as effective for roasting chestnuts, or even toasting marshmallows, if that happens to be your vice.

The ideal rural bedroom has a desk or table, preferably with a view of distant hills, at which you can write comfortably. This is a chance to enjoy your prettiest tablecloths. To give them weight and substance arrange them on toning underskirts laid over blankets. Bedroom tablecloths look best when they are floor length. And on sunny weekend mornings, you can perch a tray laden with croissants, chunky homemade strawberry jam and coffee on the table, and enjoy a civilized breakfast with your partner, away from juvenile complaints and the household chores.

Books are also a bedroom essential. Especially in guest rooms, where your visitor may otherwise languish for lack of good reading matter.

BLUES HARMONY

Blue and white is the classic colour combination for a look of innocent freshness and is evident here in every possible bedding guise. Draped on an opulent bateau lit are sophisticated examples of quilted prints, simple hand-stitched coverlets from an Indian village, a duvet cover of broadly striped linen, an Ikat, frills and Shaker simplicity.

Here you need a good mixture, to cater for most tastes – from light literature to the most refined poetry. Your own room must contain whatever is conducive to tranquillity and peace of mind. This may be a rhyming dictionary if nocturnal crosswords are part of your life. Cookery books often find a bedside roosting place, or detective novels, or the letters of Byron. Whatever is your chosen relaxant, make sure that it is within reach. No-one relishes even a minor trip to the bookcase once they have fidgeted into a comfortable position.

BEDROOM LIGHTING

So to bedroom lighting. As always, spotlights are unsympathetic to a proper country look. Bedside lamps with muted shades are kinder and just as effective. Dot table lamps about the room and use harmonizing

LEFT
TRAVELLER'S REST
Nicholas Barnard is an international authority on ethnic textiles and the bedroom of his country cottage is resplendent with African booty. The bedspread is a Ghanaian Ewe chief's strip-woven robe, and the wallhanging is a panel from a Zairean embroidered skirt. The walls are what remained after layers of paper were removed, and are decorated with stencils based on African motifs.

LEFT
ECLECTIC MIXTURE
Old and new treasures are equally at home in a seventeenth-century house – ancient beams and latch doors marry perfectly with an intricate dower chest, Afghan rugs, Indian appliqué and a patchwork quilt. The carved Austrian bed, whose painted lettering and flowers could be copied without too much difficulty, was acquired in exchange for some carpentry work. Buttermilk walls provide a kindly, cohesive background.

RIGHT

FRENCH INFLUENCE

An invitation to look anew at the colour scheme of rust against white, a combination born of oxygen and iron almost floating among ghostly white walls and floor. The sinuous chair is French, as is the curlicued iron daybed. A rich brown chenille curtain picks up the colour and echoes the curves, and an Italian mirror frames this picture of pallor. Lengthy white curtains hide the banal necessities of life.

RIGHT

ATTIC REFINEMENT

A loft bedroom full of white and light displays an elegant minimalism. Bowls and a huge wicker hamper add a human touch, the chair owes something to Charles Rennie Mackintosh, and the witty light fittings are a tribute to brown paper and wire.

shades, which you can stencil, pleat, be-ribbon or découpage yourself to suit the room. They will shed interesting and flattering light wherever need be. Candles, as everyone knows, cannot be beaten for seductive charm. Candles and firelight are guaranteed to ease the cares of the day and induce a mood of benign reverie, especially when accompanied by a glass of wine.

BEDS AND BEDDING

Pretty beds are especially important in the country bedroom. America is the home of some of the best types, including the bone-simple Shaker bed with its rope base, and the more elaborate beds with pencil posts, cannonball fourposters and serpentine canopies. There are many other bed styles, enough to satisfy every design ambition or romantic whim. However, the desire to overload the bed with an unruly avalanche of

frilled and flounced cushions is one to resist. Too many cushions on a bed can induce a contrary feeling of claustrophobia and discomfort, but cushions can be piled on window seats and in armchairs to give a sumptuous air of luxury. They offer a wonderful opportunity to make use of scraps of irresistible but exorbitantly-priced fabric, and all those squares and rectangles of exquisitely woven textiles picked up in Morocco, India or South America. Bordered with old velvet, scraps of fabric are also a handsome way of utilizing the tiny squares of tapestry that you completed before you ran out of patience.

BEDROOM SEATING

Comfortable seats make a bedroom. With a squab cushion, you can make a blanket box into a convenient seat on which to sit while fastening your shoes. A window seat can be as straightforward, but is much more seductive; the least adept home carpenter can run up a box to fit a bay window, and it just needs a cushion on top to make it comfortable enough, to give hours of inquisitive pleasure. Nothing beats ruminative staring out of the window, whether the view is of the neighbours or of ponies frisking in paddocks. And you can store bedding in the seat. Comfortably creaking wicker is the right material for bedroom chairs, rocking chairs are suitably tranquillizing and high upholstered wingbacks offer a cosy retreat.

CLOTHES STORAGE

Finally, there is the problem of clothes, and where to put them. Fitted cupboards, like fitted kitchens, are anathema to true country fanatics. A painted armoire and chest of drawers is more authentic, more decorative and may provide a good additional surface for displaying bedroom collectibles. They also offer a golden opportunity to experiment by painting auction-room finds. You can draw on the whole paint effects repertoire, with touches of gilding and a discreet use of stencils. If you enjoy it, do it. When it comes to accessories, even the most spartan bedroom benefits from the odd wicker basket, a decoy duck or a Shaker box.

SUGAR AND SPICE

An unashamedly feminine room, all pink and white, lace, chintz and roses. Such ambitions must be approached with caution — too much and claustrophobia can result. But here, the perfect balance between romance and breathability has been struck. The room looks clean and crisp, white walls bring air into the mixture, the brass bed does not blind you with its shine, and the textiles are the soft brownish-pink that results from old age.

AMISH QUILT

Unless you have severe monastic tendencies, you will probably nurse a lurking conviction that bedrooms should incorporate soft and cosy elements. While bows and frills, festoon blinds and fluffy pillows may be going too far, one does retreat to one's bedroom in quest of cuddles, human or inanimate, in the shape of big, thick blankets and all-enveloping quilts.

These days, many people own duvets, and for a while the wonderful convenience of the unadorned duvet cover eclipsed the cheery contribution of quilt or coverlet. But there is no reason why you should not indulge in everything – duvets, quilts, comforters, bolsters, pillows and luxurious quilted curtains to keep out winter if one has a mind to.

The Amish are a religious sect in North America whose plain and puritanical way of life is wildly subverted by the riotous colour of their classic pieced quilts. They continue to make a living from selling their quilts, although some of the traditional edicts have been modified to accommodate the perceived wishes of their clientele. These days they use printed fabrics, terylene wadding and cotton-polyester mixtures in place of the pure wool and cotton of the past – three developments which have made regrettable changes to the look, feel and draping qualities of the finished quilts.

Patterned fabrics used to be taboo (except used discreetly on the quilt underside), but the Amish compensated by using a vibrant, stained-glass palate of scarlets, purples, blues, pinks, greens, greys and browns and the odd touch of yellow – often set off with black. They very rarely used white in their quilts, and when they did it would never be the blank, washing-powder-advertisement white of new cotton. While the colours they used were bright, they were also subtle, and their skill in playing unexpected combinations of colour off against each other is unequalled. The strong colour and unfussy design of Amish

SCARLET AMISH

The Amish had a bravura sense of colour and design that sprang into being in the staid hinterland of America, decades before daring European painters came up with primary bright geometric art. The formula for an Amish quilt is always a simple one, with the impact coming from brilliant plain fabrics set off by black. Most designs lend themselves to speedy machine piecing. Ideally, natural fabrics are best – cotton, wool or occasionally linen, were traditional choices, and if your machine cannot contend with quilted curves and feathers, diamonds are easy to sew and are perfectly acceptable. Amish quilts were never puffy, so an old woollen blanket makes the perfect filling.

SWEET DREAMS
This Lancaster county quilt (opposite) was specially designed so that it can cover a single or double bed.

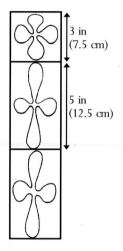

3 in (7.5 cm)

5 in (12.5 cm)

quilts give them a visual impact akin to that of the first abstract paintings of the early twentieth century. They did use brash colours, but they also used interestingly 'off' colours, and occasionally a judicious tip in tea (to achieve the textile equivalent of crackle varnish and ageing) will enhance new fabrics with a very slightly uneven aged look.

Most Amish pieced quilts consist of very simple blocks and strips, which can be copied very quickly and easily by machine. They are not large – 180cm (6ft) square is typical – nor are they thick, being often interlined with woollen blankets or felt, and finely quilted with feather vines, diamonds, tulip flowers and baskets. Hand-quilting is very soothing and pleasurable if you happen to have several years to spare. Otherwise, you would do well to cheat, and quilt by machine. The relatively small size and unpuffy filling of the Amish quilt is a great advantage here, making the whole business more manageable.

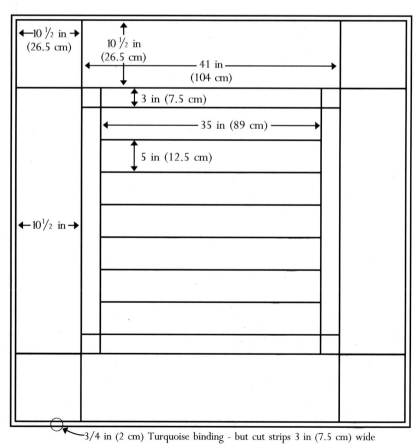

10 ½ in (26.5 cm)

10 ½ in (26.5 cm)

41 in (104 cm)

3 in (7.5 cm)

35 in (89 cm)

5 in (12.5 cm)

10½ in

3/4 in (2 cm) Turquoise binding - but cut strips 3 in (7.5 cm) wide

10 ½ in (26.5 cm)

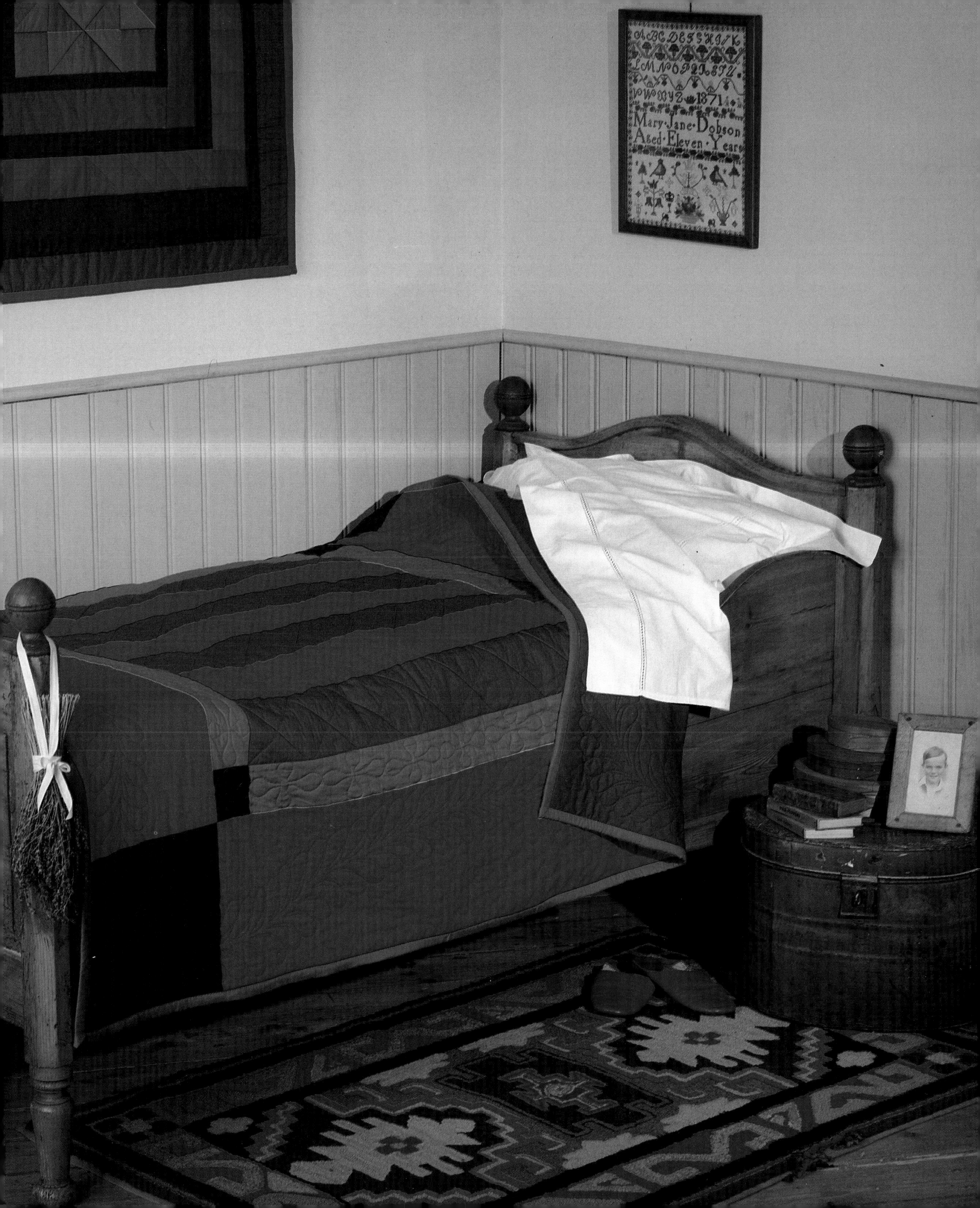
1871
Mary·Jane·Dobson
Aged·Eleven·Years

INSTRUCTIONS

Cut all pieces from 114 cm (45 in) wide medium-weight cotton. See page 126 for the cutting chart and border design templates. All seam allowances should be 0.75cm (¼ in) wide.

1 Cut four blue and three red strips (14 cm (5½ in) wide across width of fabric. Sew together lengthwise so colours alternate. Press seams towards red strips. Trim to 90 cm (35½ in) square.

2 Cut four turquoise strips, 0.75 cm (¼ in) wide, to exact length of striped square. Sew a strip to either side of striped square. Press seams outward. Cut four black squares 9 cm (3½ in) across; sew one to each end of two remaining turquoise strips. Press seams inwards. Sew to top and bottom of striped square. Press. Cut four red strips 28 cm (11 in) wide to exact length of patchwork square. Sew two strips to either side of piece. Press seams outwards. Cut four black 28 cm (11in) squares and attach to quilt as above.

3 Draw straight diagonal lines on blue and red square from corner to corner with silver pencil. Draw parallel lines from there 7.5 cm (3in) apart into corners in both directions.

4 Tape quilt outer-border design to light box. (You can improvize with a glass-topped table and a lamp.) Tape patchwork in position over design. Trace with silver pencil, holding fabric taught. Keep curves smooth and adjust so repeats join smoothly. You need to flip design for repeat. Trace corner pattern so it merges with border pattern. Keep pencil sharp. Repeat with inner-border design.

5 Prepare quilt back by cutting length of fabric 167.5 cm (66in) long and sewing two strips 28 x 167.5 cm (11 x 66in) to either side, to make a 167.5 cm (66in) square. Press. Prepare cotton bump interlining by joining a section to make piece wide enough. Overlap the two pieces by 1.2 cm (⅜ in) and join using a long, wide, zigzag stitch. There are two ways to make 'quilt sandwich'. The usual way is by tacking. Lay the three layers of fabric on the floor and smooth. Measure halfway line both ways with felt marker or thread. Spray liberally with spray glue, especially at edges. Fold quilt backing in half lengthwise, then in half the other way. Lay folds up to centre lines and gradually fold out over sticky wadding. Smooth with your hands, making sure there is no zigzag round raw edge of quilt top. Trim away excess.

6 Fill bobbin with colour to match back and needle with crimson red thread. Use walking foot to quilt diagonal lines. To start and end each line of stitching, stitch a few tiny stitches to lock. Set stitch length to about 3mm (⅛ in). Start in corners. As you get towards centre roll up quilt tightly from corners and hold with bicycle clips. Support weight of rolled-up quilt with hands and shoulders. Do not let weight of quilt pull needle. When you get to centre, turn quilt around and sew from opposite corner. Then sew diagonals in opposite direction. Finally, quilt in seam lines all round bars.

7 Replace machine foot with darning foot (or special foot for freehand embroidery) and lower or cover feed dog. Load bobbin with colour to match back and needle with crimson red thread on red and black border and turquoise thread on turquoise border. Think of the needle as a stationary felt marking pen that will 'draw' the quilt design as you move the line under it. Start by stitching a few stitches in place. Aim to keep stitch length even by running machine slowly and moving material evenly. You will have a better grip on the material if you wear lightweight rubber gloves. Sew continuously all round four sides of border, first top feathers, then lower feathers. Make sure you have room to sew complete curve before pausing. Always have the needle in the down position when you stop. After you finish sewing, rub off any pencil marks that remain on the fabric.

8 If you are not using commercially prepared binding you will need to make your own. Cut enough strips to go round quilt and join along grain of fabric – for most bindings the strips should be 7.5cm (3 in) wide. Fold in half, fold edges to centre and press.

1

5

2

6

3

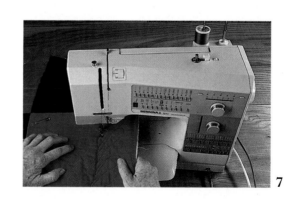

7

4

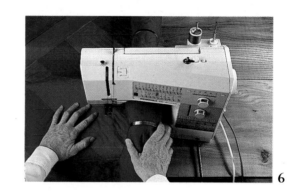

8

CHAPTER SIX

BATHROOMS & DRESSING AREAS

BATHROOM BASICS

White walls and tongued-and-grooved timber always look good in bathrooms; with a little cunning, the trim on top of the boarding can be made just the right width for accommodating all those little pieces of bathroom flotsam. A heated towel rail is one of life's great luxuries and here antique towels hang from old wooden pegs while benefiting from rising heat.

BATHROOMS &
DRESSING AREAS

Bathrooms in the country have insidiously become one of the worst offenders in the house when it comes to an overdose of melamine and metal trim. In fact, there is no reason why you should not fill your rustic bathroom with user-friendly traditional surfaces such as wood, tile and marble. Fitted bathrooms are convenient, but they lack charm. Antique plank cupboards and Victorian washstands however, are perfectly functional for storing bathroom clutter and are more in keeping with a country mood. On the other hand, large families would do best to have two small bathrooms, or a bathroom and a shower room, rather than one large and luxurious bathroom. They should both be as conveniently easy to clean as possible.

Small children and water are a fatal combination, and anything that can be left dripping wet, or strewn damply on the floor, will be. It is unlikely that you will ever manage to get a young child to put his or her wet towel back on the towel rail, but it makes sense to have more pegs, hooks, racks, shelves and rails than would seem strictly necessary, just in case a fit of tidiness strikes.

Bathrooms do not have to be business-like to be practical. It is just as easy to mop down a stained and sealed plywood floor of subtle chequerboards as it is its vinyl equivalent. We are sold all kinds of garbage with the promise that it will transform our bathing lives – all those plastic medicine cupboards with fiddly catches; those laundry bins and baskets that are too big, or too small, or which catch every passing stocking; plastic shelves for the shower which don't fit and are too depressing to bear at close quarters. Throw them all away and replace them with wooden cupboards, lockable if necessary; with light, roomy and pleasant wicker baskets for laundry; painted wooden shelves on which all your pretty packaged toiletries can sit among the shells, starfish and pieces of driftwood collected on seaside walks. Without exception, anything made from plastic or melamine-covered particle board will begin to look sad before you get it home.

Country decorating is not a momentary fad, and you want the objects with which you surround yourself to improve with time, gaining character and patina from use. Plastic cannot do this, and while it may give an air of brisk efficiency to a doctor's waiting room, it is unlikely to be the decorative ideal for your rose-covered cottage.

BATHROOM FITTINGS

Most of us are not short of material objects, we just tend to take them for granted and no longer look at them with a critical eye. Modern bath taps, for instance. From the standard chrome blob, to the enamelled Vola taps beloved of architects, none of them work as well as old-fashioned brass taps labelled simply 'hot' or 'cold' on handles you can grip with soapy hands, and fiddly bits that can be cleaned with a toothbrush. Not only do old bathroom fittings work better than anything that the twentieth century has managed to come up with, they are also elegant. Antique washbasins too were designed with beauty and practicality in mind. Their soap holders house soap effectively, their ceramic surface is easy to clean, and they were not made in an instantly passé avocado colour. Few things are quite so dowdy as the wacky bathroom suite of the previous generation. Nothing beats white ceramic and enamelled cast iron, which will look good forever and are as happy with billowing lace curtains and cornflower-sprigged wallpaper as they are with polished wood and Shaker severity.

But one can take the return to traditional plumbing too far. While antique lavatories and baths were unsurpassable in their design, their showers were not. Modern shower trays however, are available in enamelled metal and heavy ceramic which will fit in to an antiquated bathroom scheme, and if your water pressure is forceful enough, there are handsome brass showerheads to be had, with suitably simple lines. Most shower cubicles are sorry things; too small, with wobbly glass doors bearing hideous transfers or plastic curtains that stick to the wet

STONE SIMPLICITY
The honey-coloured tongue-and-groove panelling adds warmth and light to this stone-walled bathroom.

BATHROOM
COLOUR
A small tongued-and-grooved attic room has been given a spectacular paint treatment by its artist owners — the walls are roughly striped in an opulent combination of cinnamon brown and cinnabar red, and covered in paintings and ornate mirrors. The corner cupboard was colourwashed with a vibrant blue, while ornate light fittings cast a splendidly baroque glow.

body within. A slight improvement is to tile an existing alcove and fit a plain glass door to the front. Best of all are shower areas that have no need of being boxed in at all; a matter of tiling the walls and the entire floor so that it slopes gently down to a drain, making sure that you have waterproof coving at floor level all round the room. You can then use the whole room as a glorious giant shower.

If you are going to throw water around in uninhibited fashion, lighting becomes a matter for a canny electrician. In more sedate bathrooms you can replace ubiquitous spotlights and iniquitous strip-lighting with early twentieth-century fluted, coloured and frosted glass lightshades on brass wall-holders.

One must be cautious about bathroom fitments though. Manu-facturers have discovered that people will flock to buy bits and pieces

ART IN THE
BATHROOM
*If you inherit a coloured
bath, think before you throw
it out. This blue bath is
hugely enhanced by its
setting of old panelled pine,
its clever shelf crammed with
bathroom essentials, and the
misty blue of the walls. A
collection of aged paintings
and prints makes this a
civilized place to ruminate
after a hard day.*

to screw to the wall, and if you are not selective, you may end up with
enough soap dishes, extending mirrors, toothbrush holders, electric
toothbrush holders and mug brackets to look like Cape Canaveral. Most
look better in the store than they do on your wall, and should be bought
only if there is absolutely no alternative.

Bathrooms, like kitchens, need as much worktop space as possible,
enabling you to place your toothbrushes in pretty mugs. Bottles and
jars, unless they have designer labels, can lurk invisibly in cupboards.
The truly hideous bathroom necessity, men's shaving paraphernalia,
always seems to be proudly displayed. Occasionally in an exasperated
purge it might be rounded up and relegated to a basket. Other
bathroom objects are more attractive, and pretty antique bottles give a
stained glass glamour to a bathroom, when filled with bath foam.

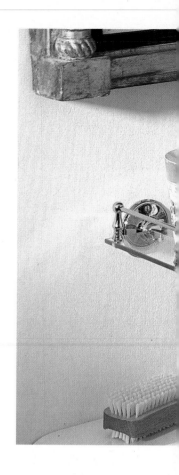

OPPOSITE ABOVE LEFT

GILT COMPLEX

*A collection of exquisite
bottles and beakers beneath
an antique pier mirror. A few
pretty objects, shown off to
advantage against white
walls and fittings ensure that
no bath need be banal.*

OPPOSITE ABOVE RIGHT

BATHROOM REVERIE

*Nostalgia with a French
flavour, from the ornate
washstand to the flirtatious
discretion of a voile screen
makes this sunny room a
sanctuary for pleasurable
ablutions.*

OPPOSITE BELOW LEFT

COBALT AND CHROME

*A positive feast of Mexican
tiles in a miniscule
cloakroom – Aztec birds and
Yucatan flowers offer a
common denominatior of
vibrant deep blue around a
ceramic basin cunningly
customized with bird motifs.*

OPPOSITE BELOW RIGHT

ANTIQUE CHIC

*For elegance and style,
nothing beats antique taps,
although they do take a deal
of cosseting to shine as they
should. This bathroom
radiates all the old-fashioned
charm of polished brass,
chintz flowers and a
lifetime's shell collecting.*

Natural materials look right in a country bathroom. Matting, tiles, painted wood or coloured linoleum on the floor; baskets of various sizes to hold clutter and clothes, wood washstands, storage and tables. If there is room, a big table is friendly and useful in a bathroom. You can pile it with books and newspapers to read in the bath; you can balance a breakfast tray on it, to sip coffee as you make up your face; you can stand the washing basket on it, as you hang a mountain of T-shirts on the rise-and-fall drier, and you can fold them neatly on it when they are dry; it can be a home for all those plants that love the steamy life. And, of course, it is a good place to bathe babies.

CREATING A COUNTRY ATMOSPHERE

The most handsome baths are rolled-top cast iron with ball and claw feet. They cost a bomb, are liable to fall through your floor, and are often too long for comfort. There is nothing so unsettling as lying in a bath, toes flexed, every muscle rigid in the effort to avoid slipping down beneath the level of the water. There is no substitute for trying out baths until you find one that is the best length for you, with the best angle for your shoulders. The bath to avoid at all costs is the coloured acrylic example which will display an unspeakable variety of embarrassing stains and marks, and will scratch at every opportunity. Whatever kind of bath you choose, it is a good idea to box it in with a generous surround on which to place your bubble liquid, shampoo, sponges and cups of coffee or glasses of wine. And of course, your candles, the ultimate tranquillizers.

A cold bathroom is a nightmare. It must have adequate heating. An open fire is a wonderful indulgence, but efficient radiators do the job just as well, and if you can find a heated towel rail that does not look like a piece of industrial detritus, it will make rising from the water as much of a pleasure as sinking into it.

There is a wonderful sense of serene civilization about a large, well-furnished bathroom. The smaller the room, the more efficient it has to be. In a spacious room you can have a cushioned wicker armchair in which to sit and chat to the person who is bathing, as well as the

RIGHT

PLASTER PINK

The walls of this new bathroom in an old cottage were prepared with a pink plaster that pleased the owner so much, he left them unchanged but for a protective coat of matt varnish. It took five strong men to lift the heavy bath into place, and the floor had to be strengthened with a plinth on steel beams to take the weight.

FAR RIGHT

A BOOK AT BATHTIME

A cultural soak is guaranteed in this bathroom whose sloping white ceiling is adorned with colourful calligraphy depicting lines from Vita Sackville-West's poem The Land.

obligatory Lloyd Loom chair piled high with clothing. You can run to a Scandinavian painted cupboard in which to put your winter clothes, or a blanket box for extra bedding. Exotically painted Indian spice cabinets are just the right size for hairpins, buttons, safety pins, rubber washers and all the other little unfindable things you suddenly need in the bathroom. A large room implies a more sybaritic use of the bathroom than mere hygiene requires. And in the thick of a demanding family, the bathroom may come to be the one place in which you can lock the door and retreat in total privacy. Everyone needs some such place, even if all they are escaping from is something as nebulous as office bickering and a querulous phone. In the perfect bathroom, you can shut the door, play some opera on the portable CD player, surround the bath with candles if you are so inclined, fill it with steaming fragrant bubbles, sip

...ST AND GREEN IN ITS LUSH FIELDS BETWEEN THE WILLOWS!

FOAMING WITH CHERRY IN THE WOODS and gone with clouds of Ladies-smock along the...

APRIL INTO MAY PASSED and still the trees wor...

THE HEDGES IN A DAY BURGEONED TO G...

THEN BROKE THE S...

The crowning of the trees' incomparably...

thickened

into heaven...

HOW SWIFT AND SUDDEN ST...

BETWEEN A SUNRISE...

...HOUGH HIS EYES
...EVER KNOW
...LAVISHLY
...FLOWERS BLOW
OTHERS
...WILL STAND
...ND MUSING
SAY

...WERE THE FLOWERS
...E SOWED
THAT
MAY

Full summer comes, June brings the longest day

How slow the darkness comes once daylight's gone

Then from the thicket sang the nightingale - so wildly sweet - so sudden - and so true - It seemed a herald from...

...GREAT BREAST SO...
WHAT CAN...
WHAT...

your champagne and forget the world outside.

The bathroom is not a good place for precious textiles. Thick curtains to keep out draughts are all to the good, but quilted ticking will look terrific and work as well as antique tapestry. Chambray, cotton checks, patchwork blocks and linen are suitable for bathroom windows. The more extrovert can explore the brilliant colours of Guatemalan and Mexican fabrics in the form of striped blinds to induce tropical good spirits whenever you take a bath. Traditional, antique and ethnic artefacts often have a charmed relationship, and carved and painted folk animals or masks from Thailand are quite comfortable with farmhouse pine and blanket boxes.

A swathe of lace, or fine open-weave cotton are good for privacy in summer. If you were feeling creative, you could even stencil a lacy fern design onto the window glass using car spray paint. Additional colour can come from painted walls decked with clever paint effects, and from stacks of bright towels, towelling robes and bath mats.

BATHROOM COLOUR

Whatever the pleasures of hygiene, most people are fairly speedy in the bathroom, which makes it a good place to experiment with strong Mediterranean colours. Bear in mind that bathroom lighting is not as subtle as elsewhere, so that whatever colours you choose cannot be as carefully modulated by low-level light. Dark colours become gloomy when there are few light sources.

The general presence of water suggests an affinity with watery colours and objects. Turquoise is not a colour that one would use freely throughout the home, but in the bathroom it may remind you cheerfully of the clean, crisp look of the adobe buildings of Greece or Morocco, whitewashed with bright cerulean and turquoise woodwork. Bright yellow is another colour to use with caution elsewhere, but with abandon near water, particularly with blue. It calls to mind the irresistible dream of sun and sparkling sea. Striped or patterned wallpapers are more sophisticated; borders make a neatly defined finish; or you can stencil shells and starfish on colourwashed walls.

GLASS AND BRASS

A tiny tattered corner of Charlestone, England, home to the members of the Bloomsbury set, demonstrates perfectly the careless conjunction of grand and battered that is the quintessence of British Bohemia. It all looks haphazardly thrown together, yet there is a method in the matching of rich yellow, copper basin, leafy curtain, and cool blue-green in the painting, together with an array of little bottles. The slight mismatch, where it occurs, adds a frisson of vitality.

CREATING MOSAICS

Mosaic has been used to decorate floors, walls, masks and ceremonial paraphernalia for centuries. Its earliest appearance was as a form of baked clay in Mesopotamia in 4,000 BC where it was used as decoration on the walls of traditional courtyard houses.

From 200 BC, the extraordinary richness and finesse of Greek and Roman floors and Byzantine mosaic arose from the growing preference for tiny glass or stone cubes, tesserae, which created a smooth, scintillating surface.

The best-known modern exponent of this wonderfully extrovert art was the Catalan, Antoni Gaudi, whose Parc Guëll in Barcelona is a sinuous, witty exercise in making much of splintered china, and whose random choice of materials is easier to emulate than the refinements of tiny tesserae. Mosaic is not difficult, but like many crafts, there is a fluent knack, almost a rhythm, which is conducive to success. Since you will very likely be making use of scrap materials at first, the answer is to start off simply by practicing on small objects such as box-lids and cupboard fronts. You will soon feel confident enough to attempt something bigger, such as a table-top, or a practical multi-coloured washable basin surround, to bring a touch of character to your tooth-brushing. You will relish the glorious satisfaction of buying chipped and cracked plates, clouded mirrors and Victorian tiles for a bargain price, and giving them a glamorous immortality by creating something entirely new.

Go for bold and simple patterns. Do not feel restricted by straight lines; the best mosaic designs are those where the main shape – and the background – flow in fluid curves, called *andamenti*. This idea, of a rhythmical flow of tiny elements, each contributing a single spark to an overall scheme, suggests similarities between mosaic and music, and in fact the two arts both derive from the Greek word *mousa*, or Muse.

PIECE WORK

The lowly stag beetle becomes a splendid thing when immortalized in shining tesserae and displayed upon a kaleidoscope of marble and bright diamonds. Mosaic is a perfect example of the whole being exponentially greater than the sum of its parts.

LEFT
SHADES OF SMALTI
Restrict your palette when working with smalti: *the combination shown here uses only tints of ultramarine with a little lemon yellow.*

The basic mosaic technique is simplicity itself. Small tesserae — fragments of a hard material — are pushed into a bed of mortar or plaster. An even quicker process is to apply the pieces straight on to a bed of thin wet glue. If you are working on a table top, you can easily fix mosaics on to a backing board of 1.23cm (½ in) plywood using PVA adhesive, grouting them later with a sand and cement mixture. Cement can cause skin burns, so wear rubber gloves when handling it.

If the mosaic will be outside, use marine plywood and glue with EVA. For the tesserae, you can use pebbles, broken tiles, pottery or coloured terracotta. But the standard mosaic unit is the *smalto*, a tiny, roughly shaped cube cut from a sheet of cooled, coloured glass.

1 For vertical surfaces, start by applying a layer of mortar, 1.25-2 cm (½ - ¾ in) thick. A standard mix is 1 part cement to 3 parts sand. For extra plasticity, instead of adding plain water, mix 1 part EVA adhesive with 2 parts water and slowly add this to the sand/cement powder to make a stiff mortar. (Use this recipe for grouting, too.)

3 Now build up the pattern using your chosen medium: in this case, smalti. *Notice how crude the design has to be to accommodate the size of the* smalti, *but also how you can mix the colours to achieve primitive effects of light and shade.*

2 You may have some visual inspiration — a post card from Pompeii, perhaps — for your design and it is very helpful to have it enlarged on a photocopier to the right size. This way you can keep referring to it for accuracy as you work. Draw your basic shapes into the mortar with a small stick.

4 In addition to the smalti, *cheap coloured limestone chippings were used — the type sold for fishtanks — pushed in handfuls into the wet mortar. They can be painted when almost dry, using thinned acrylics mixed with EVA glue. Choose colours that are alkaline resistant: earth (mars) colours, ultramarine blue and cobalt pigments.*

CHAPTER SEVEN

LIBRARIES & WORKROOMS

LEFT

MOOD INDIGO

This small library of leather-bound books and ocean trophies is a colourful antidote to the bookish-equals-brown school of thought. Indian miniatures grace the indigo walls and the cabinet has been lacquered in the colour of ripe strawberries.

LIBRARIES
& WORKROOMS

More people work from home than ever before and with the wide availability of modems, fax machines and word processors, you need never visit an office again. Painters, weavers, writers and even potters can amble out of the kitchen, coffee in hand, and get straight to work.

For those who do work at home, surroundings are crucial and subject to constant change. Your workspace will have to accommodate more books, wools, fabrics, canvas or paint than you ever intended. Workspaces have a way of creeping slowly into being. What is at first just a boxroom or part of the attic and furnished with trunks, becomes, after three years, a purposeful, dedicated and nearly efficient space. You have almost everything you need in one place, but not quite, because you probably never sat down and planned it, it all just grew.

The simplest room to address is the library, although few people have space enough for a room wholly dedicated to books, leather chairs and a large table. But that should not stop you making an area, however small, into a bookish retreat. This is often a way to utilize tall empty walls at the top of the stairs. You can build shelves up to the ceiling, find a good strong wooden ladder (country antique shops often have them) to reach the topmost books, and squeeze in a comfortable armchair. Some sort of adjustable lighting, a blanket to wrap luxuriantly around your knees, and you are all set for a Sunday afternoon spent reading. A little more available space and you could have a table at which to write and upon which to spread hefty dictionaries. Once you start bringing in typewriters, headed notepaper and a shoebox full of receipts for the tax man, the room has graduated to become an office. Mundane business things should only intrude under sufferance; a library should be conducive to enjoying books, and the fewer unpleasant connotations it has, the better it will be for your spirit.

Books are wonderfully restorative, second only to a walk along the seashore, and should be treated with love and respect. If books are your passion, then you will know by what personal radar you can track down the volume you are looking for, whether it be author, title, orange cover, or 'beside the art books'. If you have a library, it is a good idea to implement a system to facilitate the search. If you have an extensive collection, it is deeply exasperating to be standing in front of laden shelves to know that a book is there somewhere, and to have it elude you. To start with, it helps to segregate fiction and keep these books apart from everything else, so that you can always lay your hands on them. Cookery books, photography manuals and all hobby books are best kept together and close to the kitchen, darkroom or studio. If you work at home, your work reference books should be kept in impeccable order, so that you need not waste a precious minute wondering where you put the biographical dictionary or the Thesaurus. And of course, when you have finished with them, you have to discipline yourself into putting them back in the right place. It is a good idea to have ex libris stickers or a rubber name and address stamp made, so that when you lend out your books there is a slim chance you will get them back. The sort of books one lends tend to be special in some way, or people would not want to borrow them. Long after you have forgotten to whom you lent a book, you will regret its disappearance.

SHELVING SOLUTIONS

The kind of libraries that line the walls of grand houses tend to be rather daunting and not at all seductive to the interested browser. But one can take inspiration from those dozens of shelves. For a start, they are never made from Conti-board which sags between metal spurs on wall-hung strips. Real wood is the best material for shelves, whether painted or left plain. It should be used in short-enough lengths to bear the weight of hefty volumes without bending. Spur brackets and shelves are a convenient way of fitting shelves into an alcove, but they look very unfinished on expanses of flat wall. They tend to be somewhat insecure and the convenience of being able to adjust their height is something

PERFECTLY PIECED
This barn is a modern kit structure, cheaply put together and endlessly adaptable. Here, walls of shelves hold all the fabric variations for a patchwork fanatic. She can take advantage of the vast, pristine floor upon which to spread her work, while the abundant light allows her to easily check the niceties of colour, seam and pattern.

ARTISTIC LICENCE

A delicate Pompeiian frieze
adorns the walls of a studio/
gazebo. The room is filled
with small but significant
details, such as the trompe-
l'oeil *pilasters, the*
suggestion of a pediment over
the French windows and
painted flowers, roundels and
shells, with a discreet touch
of gold. In such glorious
surroundings, the call to
paint could prove irresistible.

LEFT

QUILLING TIME

A little painted desk at which only the sweetest notes are penned – a cup of Earl Grey tea in translucent china fortifies, gold rimmed specs magnify and fragrant narcissi revivify. Would that life were always this simple.

LEFT

NATURE STUDY

A tiny landing has been transformed into a workplace with a ruminative view. Varnished botanical prints adorn the doors of a provincial American bureau and rows of shells and birds bring more of the outside in.

LEFT

CHRISTMAS GILDING

Evening sunlight casts a passing golden glow upon elderly leather-bound books, a strange naive painting and Christmas preparations, giving these homely objects the richness of an antique still life.

that is usually called upon just once, when they are put up in the first place. On the other hand, if you do have a huge collection of books, it is wise to distribute some of their weight onto walls, rather than burdening all the floor joists with freestanding bookshelves. Alcove shelves can be supported very easily on strips of battening, which is a method that keeps them stable and is simple for the non-carpenter to attach to the wall.

In the library of a grand house, shelves are likely to be built-in, with neat architraves around the edges, and skirting and picture rail echoed in their construction. It is not complicated to do, and your local carpenter could achieve the same look of orderly elegance for you if you give him a drawing or a photograph as reference. An added nicety is glazed doors to protect books from dust. The fine wire netting

RIGHT

WORKSHOP BLUES
Amanda Vyvyan designs and makes furniture and her workroom is painted a heavenly blue to inspire her efforts. Tongued-and-grooved wood is an amenable and adaptable building material, giving a feeling of warmth and enclosure, which, along with big shelves, make this an inviting place to turn a leg.

RIGHT

TRAINED MODEL-MAKER
Wesley West makes wooden models for movies and commercials. His workshop is an old railway carriage - 28 tons of solidly built wood and metal which had to be moved by crane and dropped on end.

favoured by the French for library cupboard doors will keep sticky fingers at bay, and solid wood doors painted with witty *trompe-l'oeil* renditions of books will confuse everyone, including yourself, while your real books reside in pristine splendour within.

Freestanding shelving units are convenient and cheap. You can embellish them with paint, or stamped leather edgings as was once the case in the best libraries. But they always look bitty, and tend to be wobbly. Old school shelves sometimes make an appearance in auctions and bric-a-brac shops. They are eminently paintable, and ripe for any combing or dragging you may care to do.

Collections of books build up surprisingly quickly and you may find yourself buying one set of shelves after another, none of them matching, until your study has the air of a well-endowed junkyard. Besides being an untidy way to store your books, a retinue of freestanding bookshelves teetering at different angles does not make the best use of the available space. The best thing to do, if you can bear it, is to find other homes for the shelves. Look good and hard, take stock of how many oversized books you have, and work out three different book heights for the remainder. Then bring in a carpenter whose work you trust, and design entire walls of custom-built shelves, with plenty of excess room for the books you will undoubtedly acquire.

PLANNING WORKROOMS

If you work among your books, you will probably end up with a motley collection of desks, tables, filing cabinets and boxes, as well as a hefty multi-layered stratum of papers balanced delicately on top. Your desk will never be big enough, nor your files comprehensive enough and there will never ever be adequate space. A large wastepaper basket is a solution for the encroaching tides of paper that fill your heart with gloom. Labelled baskets into which you can toss bills, letters needing replies and ideas or tear-sheets — or whatever else keeps your creative juices flowing — will cut down on some of the mess and endless fidgeting with filing systems.

Have to hand all your most used and essential items such as headed notepaper, vital reference books, envelopes, pens and so on. You will probably still find that you are filing things in different piles on the floor, but at least this habit discourages visitors. In the desperate bid for efficiency, do not forget that this is a room in which you may spend much of your waking life, and attempt to make it pleasurable. At least one comfortable seat is essential so that you can sink into it when you need to think. Place some flowers on the windowsill and paint the walls and woodwork in sober studyish colours such as russets or dark blue, paired with tartan and paisley fabrics. Heavy curtains for winter evenings will add security, as will a fire. Obtain a comfortable, supportive chair to sit at when working, particularly if you spend many hours at a desk or word-processor.

LIGHTING AND FURNITURE

For lighting you can do no better than the classic shaded brass library lights which are handsome and functional in a room where frills are out of place. Surely the reason why many writers proudly proclaim that they would never forsake their Olivetti for a word processor, is that the latter, together with the entire panoply of office machinery, is extremely ugly. Fax machines, word processors, telephones and answering machines are always hideous and often take up valuable worktop space. Wall-mount anything you can and try to tolerate the rest. Office machinery may be a fact of life, but it will never look right in even the most timidly countrified interior. There is absolutely nothing you can do to mitigate its awfulness. All machines have to be accessible, proclaiming their ugliness no matter how much painted pine and stippled wall you have managed to cram into your workroom.

There is no real substitute for filing cabinets. Painting them just draws attention to their unaesthetic quality. Very occasionally you may find wooden versions that are almost handsome in a business-like sort of way. Failing that, try pushing two-drawer cabinets under a worktop or table. Or you can even make a circular tabletop to fit on to a two-drawer filing cabinet, which you can then swathe with a long circular table cloth. No-one need ever know your secret.

PENGUIN PARADE

*Books do furnish a room —
here, in somewhat haphazard
order, are the first 260
Penguin books ever published.
They make a splash of
erudite colour against the
white walls of what was once
a maidservant's room, where
any peaceful reading would
have been shattered by the
peremptory jangle of the bell.*

CRAQUELURE TECHNIQUES

The skills of the forger are not new. For centuries the skilled cabinet-maker and painter, the gilder and the carver, have set themselves exacting goals of imitation, bent on the fakery of others' work, for profit or just for professional satisfaction, for the challenge to match another's skill.

The dulling of colours, the build-up of patina, the wearing and cracking of surfaces: all these we recognize as bearing witness to the passage of time. And the most striking of these effects is, without doubt, craquelure, the crazing and fracturing of a surface either to reveal an underlying material or to act as a trap for the dirt and dust of ages. Surprisingly, given the right materials, the effect can be simplified into a conjuring trick that even the novice decorator can perform.

Craquelure is the term for an effect usually found on over-varnished oil paintings, the fine spider's web of crazing indicating that somewhere in the murky thickness of oil, layers have dried at different rates, stretching and pulling each other about.

Craquelure, as a controllable and deliberate technique, was perfected and eventually patented by a pair of mid-eighteenth-century Frenchmen, the Martin brothers, in direct imitation of oriental lacquerwork and raku-glazed ceramics that were then becoming popular in Europe. They played around with varnishes until they discovered that what was needed was a quick-drying brittle varnish applied over a tacky, slow-drying one which moved like elastic as it dried. The result was that once the top, brittle layer had dried, it fractured and split as it was carried around like ice floes on the bottom layer. Of course, it was imperative that the two varnishes should not dissolve each other, so the Martins opted for those with completely different solvents. The first was oil-based, the second water-based.

CRACKING UP
The cracked earth colours of yellow ochre and red oxide are reminiscent of parched river beds. Or you can use more sophisticated combinations of colour, like this Scandinavian blue and green, to suggest a particular region or the effects of age. Crackle paint has been used on the door and garland, and crackle varnish on the door panels.

CRACKLE VARNISH BOX

Today there are several manufacturers of crackle varnish, but it is expensive, so why not make your own? The two components are goldsize (commonly used in gilding, see pages 33-35) applied first, and gum water, made by dissolving gum arabic crystals in water. Choose a reliable make of goldsize (see page 187 for stockists). Experiment on a small piece of wood first. The technique lends a brownish, aged cast to objects and will benefit new pieces that need a little faded glory.

1 Apply a thin, even layer of goldsize with a firm brush (so that it will dry at a uniform rate). Wait until surface is almost dry but still tacky (1 - 6 hours).

2 Add a liberal layer of gum water with a soft brush. If it breaks open, the first coat is not yet ready to receive the second, so test first. Allow to dry (1 hour).

3 Use a hair dryer to accentuate cracking. Let surface cool. Rub artist's oil paint into cracks. Clean surface off and a week later apply a coat of oil-based varnish.

LEFT

BOXED IN

Wallpapers, découpage, or wrapping paper all serve as starting points for crackle varnish treatments, as their patterns and colours are easily discerned through the varnish layers.

1

2

3

1

2

CRACKLE PAINT CANDLESTICK

This is a completely different, more complex technique that involves actually fracturing a paint layer to reveal an underlying colour. A coat of crackle medium (gum water, again) is brushed over a layer of emulsion paint. When this is dry, a second layer of emulsion in a different colour is applied. You have to be quick off the mark in applying the second coat, daubing it on liberally, because its water content revitalizes the crackle medium, turning it to liquid again. It is this process that causes the movement under the top paint layer, cracking it up.

The joy of this technique is that, once mastered, it is quick and fantastically effective; and gum water is a great deal cheaper than the crackle kits on the market. On cheap furniture or toys, brightly coloured crackle paint has a simple and appealing decorative finish.

1 On a clean, dry surface, apply one coat of emulsion and allow to dry. Next carefully apply an even coat of gum water. If surface 'scisses' open, massage it gently into the surface with your finger. Allow to dry.

2 Apply a second coloured emulsion, taking care never to work over the same area twice. Cracks will appear almost immediately. When dry, reapply for a finer effect and, once finished, varnish or wax with furniture polish.

CONSERVATORIES
& GARDEN ROOMS

SUNSHINE IN WINTER

One of the great pleasures of a conservatory is being able to cheat the weather. Outside the air may be icy, but a corner in the sun can be warm behind glass – especially so when you are seated on a wildly curlicued painted cane chair, and presided over by a Victorian bust among mint and lemon-scented pelargoniums.

CONSERVATORIES & GARDEN ROOMS

People who have plucked up the courage and saved up the cash to build a conservatory will tell you that it has changed their life; that they wish they had done it sooner and made it larger. A conservatory is a room whose sole purpose is to give pleasure, and because it succeeds in doing this, it gets used for everything, from breakfast under spring sunshine, to childrens' summer parties, with the doors opened onto the garden. A conservatory can fulfil many needs, becoming everything from a painter's studio, to a writer's study, or a romantic dining room. Good natural light makes it an ideal place for fine or close work. It makes the most wonderful refuge for harassed parents and is a calm and tranquil spot in which to sip an evening Pimm's, to watch the stars come up, or to grow orchids, if that is your fancy.

Conservatories and garden rooms all have the same sort of aspirations; to make the most of the sunlight, and to extend the delights of summer for as long as possible. Garden rooms tend to consist of more glass than wall, at least along one side, and have easy access to the garden. They are a kind of no-man's-land, warm and welcoming when you have been outside too long and got chilly, and exuberantly airy after the enclosure of four walls and curtains.

The most important consideration in all cases is that of controlling heat. A glass-walled room can become unbearable in hot weather, particularly if it faces south, as so many do. A conservatory is best positioned so as to absorb morning or evening sun; facing north, it will get good, even painter's light, but will not be blistered by summer heat.

You may already have a notion of how and when you will make most use of your conservatory — lazy breakfasts warmed by the morning sun, or dining by twilight, watching the sky's darkening blush. An east or west orientation would suit these extremes respectively. The further

AL FRESCO FRUIT

In summer the garden becomes an extra room, and eating outdoors is one of the great pleasures at this time of the year. Here, roses embellish cushions, china and tablecloth in a floriferous celebration of transatlantic antique buying.

north you live, the less likely you are to be bothered by too much heat, so due south might be your favoured location. If, despite having doors and windows flung open wide, you do find that the summer glare is unendurable, it is possible to grow a canopy of vines either above or beneath the glass to give shade when you need it.

PLACING A CONSERVATORY

Obviously your choice of site will be dictated by your house and garden and the logical points of entry and exit. Another thing to bear in mind is that a room entirely composed of glass will provide no congenial wall on which to hang paintings or mirrors, and disguising a less than perfect outlook will be problematical. There will be nothing to distract from the neighbour's glass shed, the rear end of your car or the nightmarish jumble that was meant to be a herbaceous border.

Consider the view carefully. After all, you will be observing it at length once the building is in place. A conservatory in the L-shaped space between two walls gives you a place to hang pictures and wall-mounted lighting. Glazing an internal courtyard gives a positively Mediterranean air to a house and, where space is limited, an existing flat roof can become the floor of a tree-level conservatory from which you can observe the world beneath, just as the rich and glamorous do from penthouses the world over. It would be wise to ascertain that your roof is load-bearing before you get over-excited by the idea. Glazing right down to the floor maximizes the light, but it is also pleasant to have wide shelves which double as cushioned window seats. These can also disguise radiators or double as storage space for gardening implements or children's toys.

ARCHITECTURAL DETAILS

The most attractive conservatories, and those which age with the most charm and dignity, have cast iron or solid wooden frames and considered details. With such an airy construction, details are everything, and such minor aspects as finials and hinges take on undue importance. Unfortunately they also consume undue amounts of

FOOD WITH A VIEW

A kitchen/dining room extension on an old granite cottage boasts passionflowers, vines, glossy jungle plants and geraniums, all co-existing happily in the light and warmth. Floor and capacious windowsills are tiled for practicality, while vivid textiles and the transient scarlet of fruit and vegetables add a shot of colour.

money. If you are brave and bold, and have a trustworthy and imaginative builder, you can salvage original fittings from junkyards. People have been lucky enough to come upon such miracles as a set of matching cast-iron framed gothic windows which lend themselves brilliantly to re-use as a wall of glass.

New conservatories benefit from a touch of coloured, etched or sand-blasted detail. Most modern metal-framed conservatories look brutally functional and somewhat sparse. And plastic frames or glazing age wretchedly and have no advantage other than that of affordability.

COLOUR, GREENERY AND FLOORING

White was the classic colour for early twentieth-century conservatories because of the hardwearing qualities of white lead paint. But paint technology has advanced and you can now have your conservatory any colour you fancy. Any of the soft Gustavian greys, greens, blues or buffs look better than white which does not weather well and can look glaring in bright light. Cinnabar red, forest green or indigo are not overpowering on airy glazing bars and might make the perfect frame for the view.

If plants are part of the equation, you will want to be able to water and spray them without trepidation, and you will have to accept, regretfully, that muddy boots will occasionally squelch across the floor. For both reasons, most conservatories have hard flooring that is impervious to wet and dirt. Tiles are the natural choice, but marble, stone, scagolia and slate are all suitable too although they can be cold and slippery, not to mention expensive. Flat-weave kilims and dhurries can be used to soften the expanse of shiny flooring.

Herringbone brick makes an unpretentious conservatory floor, and painted or stencilled wood suits less grand interiors. Linoleum is not to be sniffed at either – it comes in good, strong colours and weathers well. It can be cut and laid to look like classic marble tiles, or given the degree of polish you feel happy with. Seagrass, rush matting or coir can stand the odd sprinkling of water and impart a sympathetic warmth to an otherwise hard and unyielding construction.

LIGHT FANTASTIC

A bright, roof-lit sunroom shows an example of Tricia Guild's legendary sense of colour and design. For her, it has a contemplative feeling, due perhaps to the subtle plaster pink walls which make a restful foil to the varied greens — the other dominant colours. The painted chequerboard floor continues a theme of clean checks and stripes.

Unfortunately, not many plants appreciate the sort of conditions that humans enjoy. The range of plants that will be happy in a conservatory is fairly limited, but suitable options include pelargonium, plumbago, oleander (very poisonous), datura, bougainvillaea and mimosa. Delicious fragrant exotica such as gardenias, stephanotis and hoya usually need conditions akin to a Turkish bath in which to thrive. Additionally, the warm still air of your conservatory is heaven for white fly and red spider mite and they are a nightmare to eradicate. Good ventilation helps, and so does putting plants outside for the summer.

GARDEN ROOM FURNISHINGS

Furniture has to be chosen with the possibility of extremes of temperature in mind. Cane and wicker chairs, rattan and Adirondack

FAR RIGHT

WORKING CONSERVATORY

A large light-filled, frost-free room need not cost the earth — here the construction is minimal: the owners have used existing walls, added brick flooring and large, simply framed areas of glass. The potting shelf is temporary but serviceable, and rainwater has been channelled for a convenient watering system.

RIGHT

EMINENCE GRIS

This quiet grey room — a surprising but successful partner to plants and greenery — is a later addition to this house. Light floods in from the roof, and the walls are plain but for unfussy sconces: the owners have simply jammed candles into light sockets, as they have with their baroque chandelier.

twig will all behave well in these demanding circumstances. Bear in mind that upholstery will fade and may get mildewed if you like to spray your plants regularly. The same applies to window shades but you can buy adhesive plastic sheets which cut down on the thermal loss in winter, and provide shelter from excessive heat in summer. Failing this, split cane, wooden French louvres, plain Holland or ticking roller blinds, can provide protection from strong sunlight.

Muslin and unbleached calico are both natural and cheap, so you can afford to experiment by hooking or tying lengths in place to best effect. There is something distinctly uncomfortable about the combination of glass walls and billowing festoon blinds: in a building whose structure is very visible and apparent, an excess of ephemeral textiles looks fussy. Simplicity is best.

Double glazing is expensive, but has many advantages in terms of heat loss and lack of condensation which can be a problem in a heated single-glazed conservatory in winter. There is a newly developed process for fusing metallic oxide onto glass, called 'low emissivity glass', which is the equivalent of triple glazing. It is a costly option though. If you have hyperactive children or need additional security, it is a good idea to investigate safety glass.

CONSERVATORY LIGHTING

Lighting is an important consideration. At night, vast areas of glass will not reflect light as effectively as do walls within a room, although reflected points of light will multiply, with a Christmassy glamour, from every pane of glass. Massed candles are particularly wonderful in a glazed interior and can be hung from glittering glass or wrought-metal chandeliers, dotted about or ranked in verdigris candelabras on a dining table. This is the place to experiment with oil-lamps – as long as there is sufficient ventilation, they can shed their nostalgic glow without choking the atmosphere. If you enjoy your privacy, you must bear in mind that after dark you will become an interesting view for any passer-by. It is a good idea to illuminate the garden outside so that you can enjoy its charm at night and feel less exposed to the outside world.

DEJEUNER SUR L'HERBE
The ultimate summer pleasure, lunch in the garden beside a tide of wildflowers. Nothing fussy, just relaxed and graceful informality - the essence of the country look that we are all striving to achieve. And in the country, your garden is a room to be exploited, quite as much as any other.

VERDIGRIS AGEING TECHNIQUES

In the occasionally damp air of your conservatory or garden room, you may well have achieved the desirably mutable colour of verdigris without trying – a close inspection of your copper pipes, bronze busts or brass hinges may reveal the beginnings of this comely corrosion whose creeping greenness you can emulate very easily on metal, wood, plaster or even plastic.

If you enjoy the gleaming result of brass polish and elbow-grease, then faking neglected antiquity will make your spine tingle with discomfort. But pause before you judge – we are not indulging in a *fin de siécle* celebration of decadence and decay here. It is a question of looking anew with unprejudiced eyes – the action of time and the elements on metals elicits wonderfully subtle colours in cloudy, painterly patches. Take your plumbing for example – hitherto, you may have pursed your lips in disapproval at the green joints intruding on the lengths of shining copper. But seen through a painter's eyes, this collision of complementary colours, is a source of inspiration.

The point is, as with so many paint effects, to create a theatrical and convincing forgery of the genuine finish – a close and careful scrutiny of the real thing is useful, to observe how the underlying metal shows through in patches, how the corrosive slats make a powdery crust in certain places, and the interesting range of blue-greens that time, water and oxygen have created.

Verdigris is a kindly finish, that quietly imparts a touch of history to your brand new conservatory accessories. It has the magical capacity to flatter most objects and colours, and once you have bequeathed old age to your plastic urn and galvanized watering can, you will find that you inspect such things as mirror frames, candlesticks, brackets and gratings with a feeling that a haphazard wash of greens and blues and whiting is just what they need to rise from banal utility.

AGED SPLENDOUR
Use verdigris as a starting point for a decorative scheme in a room and tie in architectural details like the metal railing. Sympathetic colours used on distressed plaster walls will continue the aged theme; dried flowers such as hydrangeas and lavender will add soft resonance to the crumbly green patina.

VERDIGRIS TECHNIQUES

There is a great art in choosing the right colour and transparency for your verdigris. Use emulsion diluted with water to milk thinness (about one part paint to four or five of water) and dribble it thinly on to your object with a fully loaded brush. Occasionally you can add a quick dribble of clean water for the sake of variation.

Real verdigris forms on old copper, brass or bronze, so for full effect your underpainting should emulate those materials. Old Brown French Enamel Varnish on top of metallic gold paint is a good choice. For the green sheen of old bronze, softly brush on a thin wash of dark green emulsion.

The result is an antique metal finish, a perfect ground for the quick dribble technique. Once you have used dilute emulsion paints, try mixing verdigris colours using powder paints and water, bound with five per cent by volume of PVA adhesive (use a mask when handling powders). The colours used here are whiting, viridian green and a little raw umber in varying mixtures.

LEFT

VERDANT VERDIGRIS

The lowly cistern ballcock is the real thing, all the other verdigris items have been faked with a paint finish.

BRONZE UNDERCOAT

An authentic verdigris finish depends on achieving a strong bronze underneath, so that it will glint through: stipple undiluted Old Brown French Enamel Varnish (a shellac and dye mixture) on to a layer of dry metallic gold paint.

APPLYING FIRST WASH

When dry (20 minutes later) take some dark blue-green emulsion and thin it to a milky consistency. Gently brush on a thin layer of this wash, which will spread out into a fine veil of colour.

APPLYING SECOND WASH

Let the dark green wash dry thoroughly (up to two hours), then roughly brush on a further wash of verdigris green, making sure it is thinned to the same milky consistency. Dribble more of the same wash down the surface, then dribble on clean water and washes in other colours, using white and powder colour mixes.

SUPPLIERS

GILDING

Brodie & Middleton
68 Drury Lane
London WC2B 5SP
071-836 3289
Dutch metal leaf, goldsize, bronzing powder, French enamel varnish

L Cornelissen & Son
105 Great Russell Street
London WC1B 3RY
071-639 1045
Dutch metal leaf, goldsize, bronzing powder, gum water

John Myland
80 Norwood High Street
West Norwood
London SE27 9NW
081-670 9161
Goldsize, bronzing powder, French enamel varnish

PAINT EFFECTS

Brodie & Middleton
68 Drury Lane
London WC2B 5SP
071-836 3289
Rabbit skin size, whiting, hot size glue

L Cornelissen & Son
105 Great Russell Street
London WC1B 3RY
071-639 1045
Rabbit skin size, whiting, hot size glue

John Myland
80 Norwood High Street
West Norwood
London SE27 9NW
081-670 9161
Rabbit skin glue, whiting

Appalachia
14A George Street
St Albans
Herts AL3 4ER
0727-836796
Old Village Buttermilk paints

Farrow & Ball
Uddens Trading Estate
Wimbourne
Dorset BH21 7NL
National Trust range of paints

Heart of the Country
Home Farm
Swinfen
Nr Lichfield
Staffordshire WS14 9QR
0543-481612
Old Village Buttermilk paints (mail order service)

Shaker Shop
25 Harcourt Street
London W1H 1DT
071-724 7672
Old Village Buttermilk paints

Auro
White Horse House
Ashdon
Saffron Walden
Essex CB10 2ET
0799-584888
Wide variety of colour washes, waxes and stains

Paint Magic
116 Sheen Road
Richmond
Surrey TW9 1UR
081-940 5503

3 Tarrant Square
Arundel
West Sussex
0903-883653
Specialist paint suppliers and stencil kits

Potmolen Paints
27 Woodcock Industrial Estate
Woodcock Road
Warminster
Wiltshire BA12 9DX
0895-213960
Extensive range of paints and finishes suitable for old buildings

Nutshell Natural Paints
10 High Street
Totnes
Devon TQ9 5RY
0803-367770
Water-based pigments and paints

WALL STENCILS

Appalachia
14A George Street
St Albans
Herts AL3 4ER
0727-836796
Old Village Buttermilk paints

Heart of the Country
Home Farm, Swinfen
Nr Lichfield
Staffordshire WS14 9QR
0543-481612
Old Village Buttermilk paints (mail order service)

Shaker Shop
25 Harcourt Street
London W1H 1DT
071-724 7672
Old Village Buttermilk paints

Pavilion Stencils
6A Howe Street
Edinburgh EH3 6TD
031-225 3590
Suppliers of stencils, paints, glazes and stencilling materials

Stencil Essentials
Holts Hill
Duntisbourne
Abbots
Cirencester
Gloucestershire GL7 7JN
0285-821218
*Suppliers of stencils and heat pens
for cutting stencils*

The Stencil Store
20-21 Heronsgate Road
Chorleywood
Hertfordshire WD3 5BN
0923-285577
Suppliers of stencils and materials

FLOORCLOTHS

Pine Brush Paints
Coton Clanford
Stafford ST18 9PB
0785-282799
Floorcloth paints

Cowling and Wilcox
26 Broadwick Street
London W1
071-734 5781
Floorcloth paints

Green & Stone Ltd
259 Kings Road
London SW3
071-352 0837
Artists' materials

MOSAICS

Edgar Udney & Co
The Mosaic Centre
314 Balham High Road
London SW17 7AA
081-767 8181
Suppliers of mosaic tesserae

Paul Fricker
Well Park
Willeys Avenue
Exeter
Devon EX2 8BE
0392-78636
Suppliers of mosaic tesserae

The Tile Barn
Beckford
Nr Tewkesbury
Gloucestershire GL20 7AD
0386-881122
Suppliers of mosaic tesserae

VERDIGRIS

Brodie & Middleton
68 Drury Lane
London WC2B 5SP
071-836 3289
*French enamel varnish, whiting,
raw umber, viridian powder,
metallic gold paint*

L Cornelissen & Son
105 Great Russell Street
London WC1B 3RY
071-639 1045
*Whiting, raw umber, viridian
powder, metallic gold paint*

John Myland
80 Norwood High Street
West Norwood
London SE27 9NW
081-670 9161
French enamel varnish, raw umber

CRAQUELURE
TECHNIQUES

Brodie & Middleton
68 Drury Lane
London WC2B 5SP
071-836 3289
Goldsize, gum arabic crystals

L Cornelissen & Son
105 Great Russell Street
London WC1B 3RY
071-639 1045
Goldsize, gum arabic crystals

John Myland
80 Norwood High Street
West Norwood
London SE27 9NW
081-670 9161
Goldsize, gum arabic crystals

ACKNOWLEDGMENTS

SPECIAL THANKS TO:

Front Cover: Pauline Lawton *who inspired the design;* Jane Wilkinson *for the stencilling; and* James Burnett-Stuart, Joanna Still *and* The Conran Shop *for the ceramics.*
Paints by Pine Brush.
Photographed by James Merrell.
Ann Verney *who painted the Enchanted Gazebo on pages 66, 70-71, 130-1, 148-9 and 154-5.*
Rod James *who designed the oak barn on pages 114-15 and 153.*
Natalie Woolf *who designed and painted the floorcloths on pages 102-107. Natalie Woolf can be contacted for commissions at 10 Wharfedale Street, Leeds LS7 2LF. Tel: 0532-627704.*
Kevin McCloud *for the inspirational paint and other effects on pages 32-5, 58, 61, 82-3, 144-7, 164-7 and 182-5.*
Tina Ealovega *who designed and made the Amish quilt on pages 124-129.*
Country Living's Home Design Editor Gabi Tubbs *and contributors* Margaret Caselton, Lucinda Egerton *and* Judi Goodwin *for additional styling;* Paula McWaters, Kate Haxell, Claire Worthington *and the tireless ladies in the* Country Living *library.*

The floorcloths on pages 102-3 (Jazz Wallpaper, series no. 1, series no. 3, series no. 4 and series no. 5) are copyright © Natalie Woolf, 1994. All rights reserved/DACS.

The publishers would like to thank the following for permission to reproduce photographs:

Endpapers	James Merrell,
page 2/3	Caroline Arber,
page 4	Dick Davies,
page 7	Ron Sutherland,
page 8	Tim Beddow,
page 10/11	Tim Beddow,
page 14/15	Huntley Hedworth,
page 16	Jan Baldwin,
page 19	Tim Beddow,
page 21	Tim Beddow,
page 22/23	Charlie Colmer,
page 24	*left* James Merrell,
page 24	*right* Tim Beddow,
page 25	*left* Henry Bourne,
page 25	*right* Huntley Hedworth,
page 26	Jan Baldwin,
page 27	*top* Jan Baldwin,
page 27	*bottom* Clive Frost,
page 28	*left* Fritz Von Der Schulenberg,
page 28	*right* Richard Bryant,
page 29	Ken Kirkwood,
page 31	Paul Barker,
page 32	Linda Burgess,
page 34/35	Linda Burgess,
page 36/37	Huntley Hedworth,
page 38	Richard Davies,
page 41	Henry Bourne,
page 42	Jan Baldwin,
page 45	Jan Baldwin,
page 46/47	Jan Baldwin,
page 48	Charlie Colmer,
page 51	David Brittain,
page 52/53	*Main picture* Jan Baldwin,
page 53	Tim Beddow,
page 54	George Wright,
page 57	David Montgomery,
page 58	James Merrell,
page 60	Trevor Richards,
page 61	James Merrell,
page 62/63	Martin Hill,
page 64/65	Henry Bourne,
page 66	Debbie Patterson,
page 69	Jan Baldwin,
page 70/71	Debbie Patterson,
page 72	Tim Beddow,
page 74/75	*top left* David George,
page 74/75	*top right* David Britain,
page 74/75	*bottom left* Tom Leighton,
page 74/5	*bottom right* Jan Baldwin,
page 76/77	Huntley Hedworth,
page 79	James Merrell,
page 80	Jan Baldwin,
page 82	Michael Crockett,
page 83	Michael Crockett,
page 84/85	Jan Baldwin,
page 86	Ron Sutherland,
page 89	Huntley Hedworth,
page 90	Peter Woloszynski,
page 91	Paul Barker,
page 92/93	Jan Baldwin,
page 94	*top left* Chris Drake,
page 94	*top right* James Merrell,
page 94	*bottom right* Paul Barker,
page 94	*bottom left* Clay Perry,
page 96/97	James Merrell,
page 98	*left* David Brittain,
page 98	*right* James Merrell,
page 99	*left* Rosemary Weller,
page 99	*right* Spike Powell,
page 101	Henry Bourne,
page 102	James Merrell,
page 104	James Merrell,
page 105	James Merrell,
page 106/107	James Merrell,
page 108/109	Arabella Ashley,
page 110	Frank Herholdt,
page 113	Kim Sayer,
page 114/115	Tim Beddow,
page 117	Chris Drake,
page 118	James Merrell,
page 119	Tim Beddow,
page 120	Huntley Hedworth,
page 121	James Merrell,
page 123	Tessa Traeger,
page 124	Dominic Harris,
page 127	Clive Streeter,
page 129	Dominic Harris,
page 130/131	Debbie Patterson,
page 132	A Von Einsiedel,
page 135	James Merrell,
page 136	Huntley Hedworth,
page 137	Tim Beddow,
page 139	*top left* Chris Drake,
page 139	*top right* Chris Drake,
page 139	*bottom left* Chris Drake,
page 139	*bottom right* Tim Beddow,
page 140	James Merrell,
page 141	Tim Beddow,
page 143	Jan Baldwin,
page 144	Frank Herholdt,
page 146/147	Trevor Richards,
page 148/149	Debbie Patterson,
page 150	Jan Baldwin,
page 153	Tim Beddow,
page 154/155	Debbie Patterson,
page 156	Tim Beddow,
page 157	*top* James Merrell,
page 157	*bottom* Pia Tryde,
page 158	Ron Sutherland,
page 159	Henry Bourne,
page 160	Henry Bourne,
page 163	Jan Baldwin,
page 164-167	Linda Burgess,
page 168/169	Graham Kirk,
page 170	Paul Barker,
page 172/173	Tessa Traeger,
page 174/175	Dennis Stone,
page 176/177	David Montgomery,
page 178	Huntley Hedworth,
page 178/179	Tim Beddow,
page 181	Huntley Hedworth,
page 182-185	Linda Burgess,
page 186	Jan Baldwin,
page 188	Graham Kirk

INDEX